MW00795505

Decision Cases for
Advanced Social Work Practice

DECISION CASES FOR

ADVANCED SOCIAL WORK PRACTICE

Confronting Complexity

Terry A. Wolfer,
Lori D. Franklin,
and
Karen A. Gray

COLUMBIA UNIVERSITY PRESS

NEW YORK

Columbia University Press
Publishers Since 1893
New York   Chichester, West Sussex
cup.columbia.edu

Library of Congress Cataloging-in-Publication Data
Decision cases for advanced social work practice : confronting complexity
[edited by] Terry A. Wolfer, Lori D. Franklin, and Karen A. Gray.
    pages   cm
Includes bibliographical references and index.
ISBN 978-0-231-15984-5 (cloth : alk. paper) — ISBN 978-0-231-15985-2
(pbk. : alk. paper) — ISBN 978-0-231-53648-6 (ebook)
1. Social case work—United States—Case studies. 2. Social work education—
United States—Case studies. 3. Social service—United States—Case studies.
4. Social workers—Training of—United States—Case studies. I. Wolfer,
Terry A. II. Franklin, Lori D. III. Gray, Karen A.
            HV43.D46   2013
    361.3'20973—dc23
                                    2013027815

Columbia University Press books are printed on
permanent and durable acid-free paper.
This book is printed on paper with recycled content.

Printed in the United States of America

c 10 9 8 7 6 5 4 3 2 1
p 10 9 8 7 6 5 4 3 2 1

COVER DESIGN: Jordan Wannemacher

CONTENTS

PREFACE AND ACKNOWLEDGMENTS

This project began in 2009 when Karen Gray invited Terry Wolfer to the University of Oklahoma to share his knowledge about case writing and teaching. Karen had worked with Terry on cases previously and invited him to Oklahoma to mentor faculty in case writing. He met with the instructors of Oklahoma's integrative seminar course, which uses the case method of teaching, and Lori Franklin soon joined their writing collaborative. Together, we decided to compile a collection of cases from multiple areas of practice for instructors to utilize in capstone courses, integrative seminars, and elsewhere across the curriculum.

Lori subsequently received a Faculty Enrichment Grant from the University of Oklahoma, which supported travel and supplies for interviewing practitioners for cases. In addition to this financial support from the University of Oklahoma, we also received support from faculty members at the University of Texas at Austin. Texas faculty members Noël Busch-Armendariz and Dawnovise Fowler were a part of the Oklahoma workshop and have contributed a case. Noël later invited us to Texas for an additional case-writing workshop in 2011. In these and other ways, the Universities of South Carolina, Oklahoma, and Texas have supported this case-writing project.

The cases in this collection are based on field research with professional social workers. Although these workers must remain anonymous, we are deeply grateful for their time and effort in giving interviews and reviewing case drafts and for their openness with us throughout the writing process. The interviews required that they recall and reflect upon situations they often found personally challenging, even disturbing. They were not always proud of or pleased with their responses in the situations reported but nevertheless persisted in sharing their experiences for the benefit of students. Without endorsing all their perceptions or responses, we consistently found these social workers to be caring, competent, and ethical practitioners. If they were otherwise, their cases would be less compelling. The case collection would obviously not be possible without these professionals and their deeply personal contributions.

We found most cases by asking experienced social workers about memorable dilemmas they had experienced in professional practice. In a few instances, professionals familiar with decision cases volunteered to report cases when they learned about the project. We sought cases from a variety of professional settings because we wished to provide a curriculum resource broadly applicable to social work education. For the same reason, we sought cases portraying a variety of intervention levels, including direct practice with individuals, families, or groups and practice supervision. As a result, particular cases can be used across the social work direct-practice curriculum.

We researched and wrote the cases using a highly collaborative process developed by a friend and colleague, Mike Welsh. It involved small case-writing teams led by the authors. Teams typically met for initial reporting sessions lasting 90 to 120 minutes. The case-writing process consisted of five steps. First, the case reporter prepared a brief written account of a problem or dilemma he or she actually faced in social work practice. Second, during the initial reporting session, the case reporter told the story in detail. Other team members asked questions to elicit information about the situation on multiple levels (e.g., intrapersonal dynamics, interpersonal and social relations, organizational factors, policy issues). These reporting sessions were audio recorded to collect detailed descriptions and verbatim dialogue. Third, immediately after the initial reporting session, a case writer prepared a working draft of the case that included a title, introductory "hook," basic narrative, and a dilemma-posing ending. Fourth, at a subsequent team meeting or via email, the case writer distributed the working draft to other members of the team. At this point, the team members asked further questions of the case reporter to correct, clarify, or amplify the case. Fifth, the case writer used the additional information that emerged from this discussion to revise the case. In addition, analysis from the follow-up discussion was used to prepare teaching notes for the completed case. This writing process promoted in-depth collaboration with experienced practitioners from a variety of social service settings.

The cases are carefully disguised to protect the confidentiality of the case reporters, clients, the case reporter's coworkers, and the organizations in which the cases occurred. For example, cases may be placed in other states and in organizations with fictitious names, and, of course, all names have been changed. However, in order to maintain the integrity of the cases and portray the issues and dynamics as accurately as possible, we tried to retain details such as people's ethnicity, gender, socioeconomic status, personal histories, and other characteristics that affected their interactions—keeping these details either unchanged or very close to the actual situation. Similarly, we tried to retain organizational and community characteristics.

Because some of the cases were coauthored, a bit of explanation about this process is in order. Some of the coauthors were our students or former students, and several were faculty colleagues. For everyone, Terry provided formal instruction or at least written guidelines and informal guidance for writing decision cases and teaching notes. More than other forms of academic writing, decision cases require an unusual combination of technical expertise and familiarity with practice settings. Details matter. Sometimes, for example, a decision turns on a seemingly minor fact, a matter of timing, or an overlooked policy. For that reason, it was important to collaborate with practitioners in this project.

Several master's in social work (MSW) students and graduates assisted with the research and writing. At Oklahoma, we thank former

MSW students Michelle Hovis and Danielle R. Snyder, who coauthored cases in this collection. As an MSW graduate assistant, Rachel Read contributed to research for teaching notes. At South Carolina, we thank MSW graduate assistants Laura B. Poindexter, Gecole Harley, Sean Siberio, Joe Kunkel, Brenna Healy, Farrah Willett, and Youngseong Seo, who assisted Terry with writing cases and teaching notes and with research for the teaching notes.

After completing a draft of each case and the accompanying teaching note, we solicited a review by an expert consultant familiar with the particular field of practice in which the case took place. For serving as case reviewers, we thank Amy Donaldson (Muscogee Creek Nation, Sapulpa, Oklahoma), Robin Smith (University of Texas at Austin), Jo Ann Regan (Council on Social Work Education), Linda Smith (University of Oklahoma), Mary Brandt (University of Oklahoma), Kathy Moxley (University of Oklahoma), Frank Addonizio (B & D Behavioral Health Services, Durham, North Carolina), Brett Brown (University of South Carolina), Miriam Johnson (University of South Carolina), and Lynn McMillan (Children's Advocacy Center, Spartanburg, South Carolina).

Collaboration with case reporters, coauthors, graduate assistants, expert consultants, and external reviewers helped to ensure the veracity and readability of the cases and the thoroughness of the teaching notes. We and others have already piloted many of these cases—in MSW capstone courses—and we used those experiences with discussants to refine the cases and teaching notes as well. Nevertheless, we cannot guarantee the absence of substantive errors but trust they are minor a result of these multiple forms of collaboration and review.

Finally, we thank several people connected with Columbia University Press. Executive editors Lauren Dockett and Jennifer Perillo and editorial assistant Stephen Wesley guided the prospectus through multiple levels of internal review; two anonymous external reviewers helped us clarify and elaborate the project; and copyeditor Annie Barva corrected and clarified our writing at many points.

We hope these cases will stimulate and intrigue you. More important, we hope they will provoke significant learning and growth, better preparing you for professional practice.

TO INSTRUCTORS

Terry A. Wolfer

As explained in "Introduction to the Cases," the decision cases in this collection differ from the cases commonly used in social work education. No matter what your experience with case method teaching or professional social work practice, you will probably appreciate the extensive teaching notes written for each of the cases. These notes are available for instructors at the Columbia University Press website (http://www.cup.columbia.edu/wolfer-teaching-notes) or by emailing instructors@columbiauniversitypress.com.

The teaching notes have two basic purposes: first, to help you select particular cases for class use and, second, to help you prepare to lead class discussions about those cases. To help select a case, each teaching note begins with a case synopsis, intended case use, and possible learning outcomes. To prepare for class discussion, each teaching note provides possible discussion questions and responses. These questions and responses are organized into four sequential categories: facts, analysis, action, and personal reflection. Next, the note includes suggestions regarding possible activities—for use before, during, or after the class—to supplement the case discussion. A final section identifies recommended print, electronic, and media resources.

TO STUDENTS

Terry A. Wolfer, Lori D. Franklin, and Karen A. Gray

As explained further in "Introduction to the Cases," the cases in this collection came from social workers who told us about their experiences. In considerable detail, the cases depict difficult and challenging situations these social workers actually encountered in professional practice. By both length and complexity, these cases differ from those often published as "vignettes" in social work textbooks. They are more like the situations you will encounter in your field placement or employment or you might hear about in case conferences or peer supervision.

Furthermore, these cases are like the situations you will encounter professionally in another important way: they end at a point where the social worker protagonist must decide how to respond. Traditional social work cases in textbooks often illustrate practice theories or interventions, demonstrating how something should work. In contrast, these cases depict messy, unresolved situations. As a result, they allow you to analyze the situation and decide what to do. Indeed, if you must discuss these cases or write a case analysis for a social work course, they require you to analyze the situation carefully and draw your own conclusion about what needs to be done. Your classmates and instructor may offer critique and feedback about how well your ideas might actually work in practice. This learning process may be quite different from what you are accustomed to in the classroom. Some students find it challenging, uncomfortable, and even distressing, but it closely approximates the kind of thinking and deciding that will be required of you in professional social work practice and for which you no doubt wish to be well prepared. As a result, these cases will provide opportunities for you to practice and refine important professional skills.

In addition, most of the cases report the experiences of novice social workers (e.g., students, recent graduates, or social workers with only a few years of experience). These social workers confronted situations they found perplexing and disturbing at early points in their career, just as you may in the future. Reflecting upon and discussing these cases can help you to develop professional skill and judgment in the safety of the classroom before you inevitably happen upon similar situations in the field. In short, studying these cases will introduce you to the messy world of professional practice in ways that textbooks and lectures alone cannot.

Beyond graduate education, these cases may also be used for continuing education or for discussion in supervisory sessions. Professional social workers have reported that these cases provide an appropriate level of challenge and vividly portray real-life struggles similar to those that social workers encounter in practice. Even experienced social workers will disagree about how to respond in some instances, as happens frequently in social work practice, but they, too, will benefit from discussing these situations.

Clinical supervisors may wish to use the cases in group supervision, where the benefits of group discussion can challenge and expand supervisees' perspectives, or to expose supervisees to different areas of practice. Supervisors have found them very useful in this regard, especially when a supervisee's practice experience is specialized and the supervisor wishes to enhance learning in other areas of generalist practice.

INTRODUCTION TO THE CASES

Terry A. Wolfer and Vicki M. Runnion

For more than one hundred years, social work instructors have used cases in the classroom to educate students (Fisher 1978; Reitmeier 2002; e.g., Reynolds 1942 and Towle 1954). Over time, these cases have taken many forms, ranging from brief vignettes only a few sentences or paragraphs long to complex book-length accounts.

Katherine Merseth (1996) identifies three basic educational purposes for using cases: as examples or exemplars to illustrate practice, as foci for reflecting on practice, and as opportunities to practice collaborative decision making. For the first purpose, cases provide concrete and specific examples of how professional theories or interventions apply in practice situations. As examples, cases can help students understand theoretical content and practice skills, what Merseth refers to as *illustrating* practice. During the past few decades, most of the available social work case-

---

Adapted with permission from Wolfer, T. A., and V. M. Runnion, 2008. Introduction to the cases. In *Dying, death, and bereavement in social work practice: Decision cases for advanced practice*, 1–12. New York: Columbia University Press.

books provide cases for this purpose (e.g., Amodeo et al. 1997; Haulotte and Kretzschmar 2001; LeCroy 1999; McClelland, Austin, and Este 1998; Rivas and Hull 2004). Cases have also been used less frequently for Merseth's second purpose—as stimuli for student reflection and discussion, especially regarding ethical issues (e.g., Reamer 2009; Rothman 2011). A series of casebooks by Jerry Johnson and George Grant (2004a, 2004b, 2004c, 2004d, 2005a, 2005b) incorporate commentary and questions to prompt student thinking about the issues involved. Depending on how these cases are used in the classroom, they may also provide explicit opportunity for students to practice decision making.

In contrast to cases used for illustrating or reflecting on practice, however, the case method of teaching uses cases as a site to practice collaborative decision making, Merseth's third purpose. As a result, case method requires open-ended "decision" cases, a particular type of case specifically developed for this teaching approach (e.g., Barnes, Christensen, and Hansen 1994; Christensen Center for Teaching and Learning 2011; Ellet 2007; Erskine, Leenders, and Mauffette-Leenders 2003, 2012; Lynn 1999). Such cases present students with unresolved situations that incorporate the ambiguities and dilemmas of social work practice and require active decision making on the part of students (e.g., Cossom 1991; Lynn 1999; Wolfer, Freeman, and Rhodes 2001). They describe in great detail actual situations that practitioners have encountered, reflecting the messiness and ambiguity of professional practice. Typically based on one practitioner's account, they sometimes include conflicting statements (by the various participants involved), time constraints, competing ethical values, extraneous details, and incomplete information (only what was available to the practitioner at the time of occurrence). Because the cases are open-ended, they do not tell what the practitioner ultimately did or how the case turned out. For that reason, the cases compel students to use their analytic and critical thinking skills, their knowledge of social work theory and research, and their common sense and collective wisdom to identify and analyze problems, to evaluate possible solutions, and to formulate a preferred intervention.

Decision cases were once common in social work education, including in a series published by the Council on Social Work Education in the 1950s and 1960s (Reitmeier 2002). They have recently gained renewed attention by social work educators (e.g., Cossom 1991; Lynn 1999). This book represents another set of decision cases for social work practice to supplement those published recently (e.g., Fauri, Wernet, and Netting 2008; Scales and Wolfer 2006; Wolfer and Runnion 2008; Wolfer and Scales 2006).

WHAT DECISION CASES ARE NOT

Just to be clear, it may be helpful to point out what decision cases are not. First, decision cases do not require a problem-focused approach to practice. Despite the fact that decision cases explicitly invite problem solving—in the sense of solving a puzzle or responding to a challenge—they do not require or imply a problem-focused approach to practice in the sense of having a primary focus on pathology or requiring use of a medical model. (For that matter, decision cases also do not require or imply a solution-focused approach, if that refers to a currently popular brief treatment approach.) Readers may actually assume a strengths perspective when discussing decision cases. Be aware, however, that imposing either a problem-focused or a strengths perspective can be too dichotomous (McMillen, Morris, and Sherraden 2004), distorting the reality of a case situation and potentially causing readers to overlook important aspects of the case.

Second, decision cases do not purposefully illustrate particular theories or intervention approaches. They seldom include much explicit theory, unless the protagonist mentions it. Instead, they are designed to provide detailed descriptive data about actual situations for use in case method teaching. As a result, students and instructors are free to apply whatever theories they find useful. In fact, they will usually find it necessary to use some theory to make sense of a situation and to decide how to respond. Students and instructors can draw potential theories from several sources. For that reason, to prepare for particular case discussions, instructors may (1) refer students to previous course materials or past experience; (2) assign new readings on theory or intervention approaches; or (3) require students to research appropriate resources on their own (as they must do in the field following graduation). Although case discussions seldom provide theory directly, they often clarify the fundamental importance of applying theory to practice—as students recognize the power of theory to provide a "handle" on complex situations—and provide a means for understanding and assessing the relative value of alternative theories and intervention approaches—as students propose and consider various alternatives.

Third, decision cases do not imply that social workers can or should solve a problem unambiguously, completely, and permanently for all parties. On the contrary, the best decision cases are ones about which competent, ethical practitioners will disagree. Decision cases obviously stimulate efforts to resolve problems. When we refer to resolving a problem, however, it is not to imply that all problems can be solved, but simply to acknowledge that the social worker must decide how to proceed from the point at which the social worker finds himself or herself. Further, such decision making will tend to be more effective if the social worker takes account of the underlying and interlocking reasons that have created or exacerbated the problem and addresses them in his or her decision. Increased decision-making skill is a major outcome of learning with decision cases.

Fourth, decision cases generally do not report how the case turned out. As a pedagogical tool, the open-ended nature of the cases provides powerful incentive for problem solving. It also better replicates what students will experience in practice: they, too, will need to make difficult decisions with incomplete and ill-structured information, under time constraints, and with uncertain consequences. They usually must make decisions going forward rather than have the luxury of hindsight to critique decisions by other professionals. Discussing decision cases thus emulates practice and helps prepare students for it. In short, cases provide readers with opportunities to exercise their professional judgment.

GENERAL CASE METHOD LEARNING OUTCOMES

All the cases in this collection are decision cases. Properly used, they provide opportunities for the general types of learning associated with case method discussions. As suggested by Louis Barnes, Roland Christensen, and Abby Hansen, decision cases help students to adopt at least six aspects of a professional practitioner's point of view: (1) "a focus on understanding the specific context"; (2) "a sense for appropriate boundaries"; (3) "sensitivity to interrelationships"; (4) "[examination] and understanding [of] any . . . situation from a multidimensional point of view"; (5) "[acceptance of] personal responsibility for the solution of organizational problems"; and (6) "[a]n action orientation" (1994, 50–51). Writing as business educators, these authors argue that case method instruction helps to develop in students an applied, "administrative point of view" (50). The concept of an administrative or practitioner point of view shifts attention from what students know to how they can use their knowledge. We refer to this point of view as "thinking like a social worker" and elaborate on it here.

First, the cases provide ample detail about the background and context of the practice situations they depict. As students wrestle with the practice dilemmas in these cases, they come to understand the critical significance of context for problem framing and intervention. The relevant context varies across cases. For example, in particular cases the context will include some combination of culture, law, policy, society, community, and organization. Many of the cases also include specific dates because timing—whether internally (relative to events within the case) or externally (relative to events in the broader environment)—is another important aspect of context. But not all the details turn out to be significant. Just as they must do in actual practice situations, students (social workers in training) must sort through the contextual information, selecting what is relevant and significant and disregarding what is not. Addressing the case dilemma occasionally requires gathering information not provided in the case because overlooking some aspect of context may have contributed to the practitioner's dilemma. Discussing these cases provides opportunities to practice deciding what is relevant and incorporating selected information into problem formulations and subsequent interventions.

Second, appropriate handling of the contextual information will require clear delineation of boundaries, sorting out what is separate and what is related. As students wrestle with the practice dilemmas in these cases, they come to appreciate the need to distinguish aspects of situations. For example, many of the cases turn on proper distinctions between social workers and clients, between individual clients and their families, between children and parents (or other adults), between professions, or between organizations. Sometimes these boundaries do not seem apparent to the protagonist. In fact, lack of clarity regarding boundaries often contributes to the reported dilemmas. Of special importance, some cases cannot be resolved without specifying the client system (and practitioners may disagree about this). In some practice settings, for example, the commitment to considering patients' families as part of the client system sometimes obscures the boundaries between patients and their families, creating dilemmas for social workers. Likewise, social workers must consider whether addressing a particular client need falls within the scope of their employing organization's mission, license, expertise, and priorities. As suggested earlier, discussing these cases provides opportunities for students to practice identifying and taking account of such boundaries in concrete situations.

Third, students must consider the webs of relationships present in these cases in addition to the cases' background or context and the boundaries between subsystems. The cases portray relationships on multiple levels. For example, they quite concretely depict relationships within families, professional work teams, and organizations. These human relationships reflect the subtleties of cognition, emotion, motivation, and behavior. Many of the cases include both spoken and internal dialogue to portray more fully how the social workers who reported the cases experienced these situations and relationships. More abstractly, the cases also depict relationships between programs and policies, between professionals and host organizations, between events and their temporal context, and between theory and practice. In general, the cases require that students interpret the "raw" data provided in order to draw their own conclusions. Where the cases include assumptions held or conclusions drawn by the protagonist or other persons in the case, students must decide what to accept. Such assumptions and conclusions always shape how people understand situations, and they sometimes contribute to the problem.

Relationships serve not only as background for the cases. Several cases also reflect the evolution over time of helping relationships (with individuals, families, or groups) or professional relationships (in supervision, interdisciplinary conferences, or work teams). Readers may sometimes want to dismiss particular cases by saying they would not have made the mistake that contributed to the case dilemma. But thoughtful readers will realize that such mistakes are often clearer in hindsight and that they cannot wish problems away. No matter who or what contributed to the current dilemma, the social worker must decide what to do next. There is no opportunity to go back in time to revise these relationships; change is only possible going forward.

Fourth, although all the cases were based on interviews with individual social workers, they do not provide information from only the protagonist's perspective. As much as possible, the case-reporting interviews explored perspectives held by other participants. Even though this information was inevitably filtered through the eyes and ears of the social worker protagonist, it provides other perspectives on the case situations. It is portrayed by dialogue most often, but also sometimes by written reports and email. In whatever form, this information reflects differences in perspective and invites interpretation. Readers will need to interpret the information itself as well as the protagonist's reasons for recalling and reporting it.

Fifth, the cases demonstrate social workers' essential roles. Each case poses one or more dilemmas experienced by the social worker who reported the case, highlighting his or her critical roles as decision maker and actor. The reporting social worker was often the only person who could intervene in the particular situation. Choosing not to intervene was seldom a real option and would carry its own consequences. Furthermore, the social worker often labored under time pressure and with incomplete information because some imminent event required his or her decision and intervention. As much as possible, the cases attempt to provide full information about the context for decision making (i.e., personal, professional, organizational, policy factors) of which the social worker was aware at the time. But that means each case also deliberately omits information that was not available to the social worker at the time.

In addition, many of the cases implicate the social workers themselves in the decision-making context. In other words, these detailed cases often reflect how the social workers' personal background, professional training, previous work experience, and time on the current job may have contributed to their preparation and ability to respond. More specifically, the cases reflect how the social workers' personalities, values, ethics, knowledge, and skills influenced their decision making.

Discussing these cases will help students understand how their own personalities, values, ethics, knowledge, and skills limit, focus, or enhance what they can understand and decide in particular cases. In short, reading and discussing these cases will help students better understand how the social worker's self affects professional practice.

Sixth, the cases also clarify the necessity of moving from analysis to action. Whether the information appeared complete and clear, the social workers had to make decisions and act. In many cases, the situation could not wait. For example, a person was in crisis, or some other deadline was looming, which left limited time for deciding and then for intervening. As suggested earlier, not deciding or intervening is also a kind of intervention, with its own set of consequences, and should be chosen just as carefully as any more active intervention rather than by default. At the same time, the case discussions often explore the potentially harmful consequences of ill-considered or precipitous action. In that way, discussion of these cases can help students to understand the fundamental necessity of intervening and the importance of doing so based on thorough analysis of available data.

MORE SPECIFIC LEARNING OUTCOMES

In addition to helping students to learn to "think like a social worker"—skills that are vital in any area of social work practice—the cases provide a vehicle for students to develop their understanding of particular fields of practice (e.g., international adoption, geriatric psychiatry, military social work). Although case method teaching in general is intended to help students integrate and apply knowledge they already have, it also, like actual practice, often requires students to identify gaps in their knowledge and take steps to fill those gaps, under similar time pressures.

Social work as a profession is concerned with systems and boundaries and especially with conflicts between and among them. Social workers in these cases interact with professionals from other disciplines—including nursing, medicine , law enforcement, ethics committees, education, and administration, for which the financial bottom line is the final determinant of a decision—and organizational cultures—including hospitals, public schools, residential treatment centers, a university, social service agencies, and courts. The social workers must decide how to handle a range of conflicts among and with clients, coworkers, supervisors, supervisees, and administrators. Although the cases do not always identify specific ethical principles, concepts such as autonomy, beneficence, nonmaleficence, informed consent, quality of life, and justice serve to inform or heighten the dilemmas presented. The social workers are faced with questions, for example, about whether a client has the capacity to make important decisions about his or her care at multiple points through the course of illness, about who should determine what is best for a client, and about the meaning of quality of life or suffering when the client cannot clearly communicate his or her own perspective.

As is true in all social work practice settings, social workers in these cases have to grapple with the integration of and conflicts between their personal and professional lives. Some must decide how to handle their discomfort with or dislike of a client or coworker or, conversely, their identification with, admiration for, and possibly even friendship with a client or coworker. Others must deal with their own past trauma in order to know how to help their clients deal with trauma and with their own grief in order to know how to help their clients grieve.

Finally, social workers must deal with their own beliefs about and responses to pain, suffering, illness, disability, stigma, prejudice, alienation, and grief. They need to be keenly aware of the ways in which their own personal histories may either hinder their work with or serve as a resource for clients in similar circumstances. And they need to be aware of the ways in which their exposure to their client's issues affects them, both as professionals and as human beings.

DIVERSITY WITHIN THE COLLECTION

We originally wrote the cases in this collection for use in MSW capstone courses at the University of South Carolina, the University of Oklahoma, and the University of Texas at Austin. For that reason, most of the cases come from those regions of the United States and reflect regional demographics. Nevertheless, we sought diversity on a variety of demographic dimensions (e.g., gender, age, race/ethnicity, socioeconomic status, sexual orientation, religion, immigrant status).

Case settings	Inpatient mental health	Residential care	Outpatient medical clinic	Schools	Outpatient mental health	University campus	Refugee resettlement	International adoption	Veteran's Administration	Child protective services	Hospice	Domestic violence	Inpatient medical care
15. "Don't tell her"	×										×		×
14. Driven to Drink		×											
13. Nowhere to Skate					×								
12. Exposed	×												
11. Matter of Life and Death										×			
10. Wandering										×			
9. Private, Dismissed					×				×				
8. Flying Flags					×								
7. I'm a Social Worker				×									
6. Child Collectors								×					
5. MSW Internship Thing							×						
4. Believing Women						×							
3. But Someone Could Die!		×								×		×	
2. Gay-For-Pay					×								
1. No Place Like Home	×												

	Client system					
		• Individual	• Family	• Group	• Supervisee/Colleague	• Program/Organization
15. "Don't tell her"		×	×			
14. Driven to Drink					×	
13. Nowhere to Skate		×	×			
12. Exposed		×	×			
11. Matter of Life and Death			×		×	×
10. Wandering			×		×	×
9. Private, Dismissed		×				
8. Flying Flags				×	×	
7. I'm a Social Worker		×		×		×
6. Child Collectors			×			
5. MSW Internship Thing					×	
4. Believing Women		×				
3. But Someone Could Die!		×	×			×
2. Gay-For-Pay				×		
1. No Place Like Home		×	×			

Populations at risk	• Elderly	• Children	• Women	• Racial/ethnic minorities	• Sexual minorities	• Developmental disabilities	• People in poverty	• Immigrants/refugees	• People with mental illness	• People with physical illness	• Veterans	• Children in state custody	• Trauma survivors
1. No Place Like Home	×		×	×			×		×				
2. Gay-For-Pay		×			×							×	×
3. But Someone Could Die!		×	×			×	×					×	×
4. Believing Women			×						×				×
5. MSW Internship Thing								×					
6. Child Collectors		×	×			×	×						
7. I'm a Social Worker		×	×			×							
8. Flying Flags									×		×		×
9. Private, Dismissed			×	×	×				×			×	×
10. Wandering		×	×				×					×	
11. Matter of Life and Death		×	×			×	×					×	
12. Exposed		×							×				
13. Nowhere to Skate		×										×	
14. Driven to Drink		×	×									×	
15. "Don't tell her"	×									×			

Case	Client competence	Autonomy/self determination	Informed consent	Confidentiality	Quality of life	Duty to warn/protect	Professional collegiality	Professional competence	Colleague impairment
15. "Don't tell her"	X	X	X		X				
14. Driven to Drink						X	X		X
13. Nowhere to Skate	X					X	X		
12. Exposed					X				
11. Matter of Life and Death						X	X	X	
10. Wandering				X	X				
9. Private, Dismissed		X			X				
8. Flying Flags							X		
7. I'm a Social Worker								X	
6. Child Collectors	X	X							
5. MSW Internship Thing							X	X	
4. Believing Women	X								
3. But Someone Could Die!	X	X			X				
2. Gay-For-Pay						X	X		
1. No Place Like Home	X	X	X	X	X				

Ethical issues: • Client competence • Autonomy/self determination • Informed consent • Confidentiality • Quality of life • Duty to warn/protect • Professional collegiality • Professional competence • Colleague impairment

	Technical knowledge												
	• Discharge planning	• Home study processes	• Individualized education plans	• Military sexual trauma	• PTSD	• Reunification planning	• Rape/domestic violence	• Traumatic brain injury	• Colleague impairment	• End of life	• Suicide/self-harm assessment	• Practice with LGTBQ youth	• Legal issues
15. "Don't tell her"										X			
14. Driven to Drink									X				
13. Nowhere to Skate											X		
12. Exposed	X										X		
11. Matter of Life and Death		X											X
10. Wandering						X							X
9. Private, Dismissed				X	X								
8. Flying Flags					X								
7. I'm a Social Worker			X										
6. Child Collectors		X											X
5. MSW Internship Thing													X
4. Believing Women				X			X						
3. But Someone Could Die!				X			X	X					
2. Gay-For-Pay												X	
1. No Place Like Home	X												X

The cases involve varying client system levels and ecological contexts. In addition, we included many fields of practice and incorporate a variety of ethical, technical, and professional issues. The case matrix given here identifies selected dimensions of the decision cases and reflects their diversity and complexity.

Although these decision cases include people from a relatively limited range of demographic and cultural groups, what students learn about particular diversities may be secondary to what they learn about how to take account of these diversities in professional practice. In other words, though content knowledge is necessary, it is not sufficient for decision making in these cases or in professional practice. Students can learn to take account of diversity by dealing with familiar as well as unfamiliar types of diversity. For example, thought experiments that consider how a case might differ if some demographic element were substituted can be enlightening.

We trust this collection of decision cases will provide stimulating and challenging opportunities for students to practice professional social work decision making. The cases may provide new information about various aspects of professional social work practice. At times, the learning that results from discussing these cases may be somewhat uncomfortable and difficult—perhaps even distressing. We trust, however, that it will better prepare students for professional social work practice.

REFERENCES

Amodeo, M., R. Schofield, T. Duffy, K. Jones, T. Zimmerman, and M. Delgado, eds. 1997. *Social work approaches to alcohol and other drug problems: Case studies and teaching tools.* Alexandria, VA: Council on Social Work Education.

Barnes, L. B., C. R. Christensen, and A. J. Hansen. 1994. *Teaching and the case method.* 3rd ed. Boston: Harvard Business School Press.

Christensen Center for Teaching and Learning. 2011. Case method in practice. Harvard Business School, http://www.hbs.edu/teaching/case-method-in-practice/.

Cossom, J. 1991. Teaching from cases: Education for critical thinking. *Journal of Teaching in Social Work* 5 (1): 139–155.

Ellet, W. 2007. *The case study handbook: How to read, discuss, and write persuasively about cases.* Boston: Harvard Business School Press.

Erskine, J. A., M. R. Leenders, and L. A. Mauffette-Leenders. 2003. *Teaching with cases.* 3rd ed. London, Canada: Ivey and University of Western Ontario.

——. 2012. *Learning with cases.* 4th ed. London, Canada: Ivey and University of Western Ontario.

Fauri, D. P., S. P. Wernet, and F. E. Netting. 2008. *Cases in macro social work practice.* 3rd ed. Boston: Allyn & Bacon.

Fisher, C. F. 1978. Being there vicariously by case studies. In M. Ohmer and Associates, eds., *On college teaching: A guide to contemporary practices*, 258–285. San Francisco: Jossey-Bass.

Haulotte, S. M. and J. A. Kretzschmar, eds. 2001. *Case scenarios for teaching and learning social work practice.* Alexandria, VA: Council on Social Work Education.

Johnson, J. L., and G. Grant Jr. 2004a. *Adoption.* Boston: Allyn & Bacon.

——. 2004b. *Medical social work.* Boston: Allyn & Bacon.

——. 2004c. *Mental health.* Boston: Allyn & Bacon.

——. 2004d. *Substance abuse.* Boston: Allyn & Bacon.

——. 2005a. *Community practice.* Boston: Allyn & Bacon.

——. 2005b. *Domestic violence.* Boston: Allyn & Bacon.

LeCroy, C. W. 1999. *Case studies in social work practice.* 2nd ed. Pacific Grove, CA: Brooks/Cole.

Lynn, L. E., Jr. 1999. *Teaching and learning with cases: A guidebook.* New York: Chatham House.

McClelland, R. W., C. D. Austin, and D. Este. 1998. *Macro case studies in social work.* Milwaukee: Families International.

McMillen, J. C., L. Morris, and M. Sherraden. 2004. Ending social work's grudge match: Problems versus strengths. *Families in Society: The Journal of Contemporary Social Services* 85 (3): 317–325.

Merseth, K. K. 1996. Cases and case methods in teacher education. In J. Sikula, T. J. Buttery, and E. Guyton, eds., *Handbook of research on teacher education*, 2nd ed., 722–744. New York: Simon & Schuster Macmillan.

Reamer, F. G. 2009. *The social work ethics casebook: Cases and commentary.* Washington, DC: NASW Press.

Reitmeier, M. 2002. Use of cases in social work education. Unpublished manuscript, University of South Carolina, Columbia.

Reynolds, B. C. 1942. *Learning and teaching in the practice of social work.* New York: Farrar & Rinehart.

Rivas, R. F. and G. H. Hull. 2004. *Case studies in generalist practice.* 3rd ed. Belmont, CA: Brooks/Cole.

Rothman, J. C. 2011. *From the front lines: Student cases in social work ethics.* 3rd ed. Boston: Allyn & Bacon.

Scales, T. L. and T. A. Wolfer, eds. 2006. *Decision cases for generalist social work practice: Thinking like a social worker.* Pacific Grove, CA: Brooks/Cole—Thompson Learning.

Towle, C. 1954. *The learner in education for the professions: As seen in education for social work.* Chicago: University of Chicago Press.

Wolfer, T. A., M. Freeman, and R. Rhodes. 2001. Developing and teaching an M.S.W. capstone course using case methods of instruction. *Advances in Social Work* 2 (2): 156–171.

Wolfer, T. A. and V. M. Runnion. 2008. *Dying, death, and bereavement in social work practice: Decision cases for advanced practice.* New York: Columbia University Press.

Wolfer, T. A. and T. L. Scales, eds. 2006. *Decision cases for advanced social work practice: Thinking like a social worker.* Pacific Grove, CA: Brooks/Cole—Thompson Learning.

Decision Cases for
Advanced Social Work Practice

I

NO PLACE LIKE HOME

Lori D. Franklin

Medical social worker Sandy Deloach located Lucy Haskins in the TV room and sat down across from her. Lucy was a sixty-three-year-old patient on the Geriatric Psychiatric Services Unit at Durant Regional Health Services.

"Lucy, great news," Sandy began. "We're going to discharge you soon. Have you given any more thought to where you would like to go?"

"To my daughter's." Lucy's tone was flat, and her voice quiet.

"Lucy," Sandy said calmly, "remember, we told you we spoke with her and she said no. You can't go back there."

Development of this decision case was supported in part by funding from the School of Social Work at the University of Oklahoma. It was prepared solely to provide material for class discussion and not to suggest either effective or ineffective handling of the situation depicted. Although the case is based on field research regarding an actual situation, names and certain facts may have been disguised to protect confidentiality. The author thanks the anonymous case reporter for cooperation in making this account available for the benefit of social work students and instructors.

"She says stuff like that, but she'll let me. Just get me back there, and it will be okay."

"Lucy," Sandy said, "your daughter said you couldn't come back this time."

"It will be fine," Lucy spoke evenly. "Just take me to my car, and I'll get there myself then."

"Lucy, your car really isn't a safe place for you right now." Sandy felt herself getting frustrated. "It's summer, and it's hot out. It's too hot to be in a closed-up car. And your car isn't working."

"That's okay, I don't need housing. I just like it with my daughter. And if she doesn't want me, it's okay in the car. I'll figure it out; I've done it before."

DURANT REGIONAL HEALTH SERVICES

Durant Regional Health Services (DRHS) was the largest hospital in southeastern Oklahoma and housed the only inpatient psychiatric unit for the elderly in that area. Typical patients of its rural service area generally had much lower income than the rest of Oklahoma. Many of the patients were on Medicaid or had no pay source at all. The hospital had a full range of general medical services, including inpatient mental health care, but the Geriatric Psychiatric Services Unit (GPSU) was the only "specialty" service the hospital offered.

In 2008, DRHS faced many challenges as a for-profit hospital. The large hospital was often under capacity, and these vacancies created a strain on profits. Many of the patients in this rural area of the state lived in poverty. They did not qualify for Medicaid, so their medical services were not reimbursed. The large indigent population had always strained emergency care services, utilizing the emergency room as a source of primary care, and reimbursement for these services was very low. The hospital often sacrificed profits when serving low-income patients without a pay source yet had to provide emergency medical care for all patients in need. Many of these patients were treated in the emergency room and discharged and did not utilize other hospital services. But the hospital was for profit, so it relied heavily on insured patients and the income-generating units that served them in order to stay afloat.

THE GPSU

The GPSU was a successful unit in terms of reimbursement rates. The hospital's chief financial officer had referred to the GPSU in open meetings as "our greatest revenue producer" and part of the reason the hospital could stay open. Most of the geriatric clients were either on disability or Medicare, which obviously led to a higher rate of reimbursement than units that primarily served the indigent population. But even though the rates of reimbursement were high, the unit had twelve rooms, and the daily census was usually only seven or eight patients. The staff was adequate for this census and spent a great deal of time with patients individually and in group work.

The unit itself had a homey appearance, despite being a locked unit. It was rectangular, with two long hallways of individual patient rooms on each side and locked doors at either end. In the middle, there was a nurses' station, group rooms, and a kitchen and dining room. The floor was nicely carpeted, and there were comfortable couches and rocking chairs in the common areas. The chairs were vinyl and easy to clean, but they were not attached to the floor and had decorative floral prints.

The staff on the geriatric unit were very experienced and worked well together as a supportive team. The program was directed by Marjorie Adams, a licensed clinical social worker (LCSW) who had almost twenty years of experience working with the elderly. The outpatient social worker, Pam Carson, was an experienced LCSW who was a mentor to the staff. Sandy Deloach, MSW, was the discharge planner. The professional team also included two geriatric certified nurses, a recreation therapist, and a psychiatrist. They all got along well and seemed to respect each other as people and as professionals.

SANDY DELOACH

Before Sandy Deloach began working at the hospital, she had spent ten years in sales at a large company and found herself enjoying a nice income, but not feeling much satisfaction in her work. She decided to make a dramatic career change and pursue a bachelor's and then a master's degree in social work.

Sandy's marketing background helped her get her foot in the door, and she was hired in DRHS's Community Relations Department while she began work on a bachelor's degree. She was able to do a bachelor's field practicum in the GPSU while still employed in the Community Relations Department, and Pam Carson had been her practicum supervisor. Sandy was organized and efficient, so she managed the difficult schedule of a full-time marketing job, coursework, and the practicum. A paid position in discharge planning became available as she finished the bachelor's degree, so she happily applied, was hired, and left marketing behind. Even though the job was technically a master's level position, her performance record was such that the hospital made an exception and hired her with a bachelor's degree, knowing that she had plans to pursue an MSW. The position served as her master's field practicum, and after graduating in May 2008, she kept the job.

Sandy had now been out of school for almost two months but had been at the hospital for nearly five years. She was glad to have the stability of the now familiar job as a discharge planner. She enjoyed her job and loved knowing she was helping people instead of just selling products. Her husband was also in marketing, so her family was able to endure the reduced income that came with her career change. She cared about her elderly clients and took pride in helping those who desperately needed services.

DISCHARGE PLANNING . . . AND MORE

Sandy's job title was officially "discharge planner," but the small unit worked closely as a team, and she did many different things on the unit. Now that Sandy had her MSW, Marjorie assigned her not only psychosocial assessments and discharge planning, but some group therapy as well. She ran a daily group that focused on cognitive and recreational therapy. This group was challenging to lead because the unit accepted patients with a wide range of levels of functioning. If group participants were higher functioning, they would do more traditional group therapy, focusing on the cognitive patterns associated with depression or behavioral concerns using a cognitive-behavioral model. On those days, the patients interacted with each other, and Sandy often saw real changes as they realized how their relationships and thinking patterns affected their moods.

But on other days if group participants were more cognitively impaired, she kept the groups more activity oriented. For example, patients might toss a beach ball while saying their favorite color or do some other type of group activity. These group sessions were less satisfying to her, but at least she was working toward engaging the patients in something. Many of the geriatric patients suffered with dementia and other conditions that reduced awareness of their surroundings, so any progress in connecting them to others was a success.

It was more difficult, though, to handle a mix of cognitive levels in the group or when a patient had severe anxiety or another condition that impaired his or her ability to participate or interact. The wide variation of cognitive functioning as well as the continual turnover of an inpatient environment made it nearly impossible to follow a curriculum or plan ahead for group. When the group was mixed, Sandy would often divide the group into a cognitive therapy group and a recreational therapy group. She could then have the recreational therapist work with the lower-functioning group and do some activities geared toward their abilities. It was difficult to decide how to divide the group, though. Sandy would begin with an analysis of the scores on the Mini Mental Status Exam, the Geriatric Depression Scale, and the general assessment. But making the division was always more complicated than that because many people were not clearly cognitively impaired yet still didn't seem appropriate for an insight-oriented group. So she sometimes would ask the recreational therapist to cofacilitate with her, and they would try to tailor the group to the needs that emerged.

Sandy's job as a discharge planner was also becoming increasingly complicated. With new patients, her approach was to start planning for discharge from the very beginning. When she first began, it seemed as if most of the discharge plans were to nursing homes or assisted-living facilities, or patients just returned to the family members who had brought them to the hospital. Most patients were not voluntary but arrived with adult protective services or with family members who had durable power of attorney. Some were referred by nursing homes and hospitals. There were many with Alzheimer's disease and other kinds of dementia. Perhaps a third of the patients had some kind of chronic depression. Sometimes patients were there because of a suicide attempt, but many were there because of ongoing symptoms of mental illness that interfered with the ability to care for themselves.

For involuntary patients detained against their will on an emergency basis, the unit had seventy-two hours to assess the patient's needs and initiate treatment. After seventy-two hours, the patient would be released if there was no court order to continue the detention. To obtain a court order, Sandy would write a petition to the court, which generally included a description of how the patient presented to the unit, details of specific behaviors, past and current diagnoses, and a summary of assessment results. She wrote the petitions, and then the psychiatrist, Dr. Hamilton, whom she kept informed of patient information, signed them. The unit enjoyed good relationships with most of the county courts, so Sandy's recommendations on the petitions were usually honored. A court order to continue detention gave the unit additional time to stabilize a patient's condition and Sandy time to create a robust discharge plan that would fully address the patient's needs.

Sandy usually had some idea at intake about where the patient would go at discharge. But lately there seemed to be more patients trickling through with more complicated situations. The unit had always defined "geriatric" as fifty-five and older, but now some patients in their early fifties or even late forties were coming to the unit. Some came with no family connections, no stable housing, and increasingly severe mental illnesses. In the past, patients stayed an average of ten days, but more and more this set period didn't seem to be enough time to stabilize the patients. Sandy was used to getting them in, completing the psychosocial assessment within three days, putting services into place for the family within five days, and preparing the discharge plan. But the more severe patients took more staff time and were more difficult to place. Sandy also felt pressure to move faster as the number of vacant beds on the unit gradually decreased.

ADMITTING LUCY

Arriving at work on Monday morning, Sandy looked over the chart of Lucy Haskins as she prepared to meet with Lucy for her initial assessment. Lucy had been admitted during the night shift, so Sandy hadn't got to meet with her from the beginning, as she would have preferred. She stopped at the nurse's station to speak with Cynthia Crowder, who was just ending her night shift. Cynthia was the head nurse on the unit and had admitted Lucy when the police brought her in.

"Cynthia," Sandy asked, "I know you're on your way out, but could you bring me up to speed quickly on Lucy Haskins?"

"Sure," Cynthia said, "the police brought her in last night, and she was really upset. The police said, 'Boy, you sure got a live one there, good luck,' when they dropped her off. The police said she was found wandering around on the highway, and when they tried to talk to her, she started throwing rocks at them. The police said it took three of them to restrain her and get her in the car, so she was in handcuffs when she got here, of course."

"What did the police say she was like once they got her in the car?" Sandy asked.

"She was really angry and was yelling things like, 'This is bullshit, and you should be arresting my daughter!' It sounds like Lucy had been staying with her daughter, and then they had a big fight. The police report says that Lucy threatened her daughter with a knife, broke a window, and kicked a hole in the wall. Then she drove off in her car, but it broke down outside of Hugo, and that's when the police found her wandering around on the highway."

"Hugo is in Choctaw County, though," Sandy said, puzzled. "I guess they had to bring her here to Bryan County because no hospital out that way could help her. We sure are getting folks from far and wide lately, aren't we? I see she's just sixty-three, too."

"Well, I guess we have room for her," Cynthia stated. "She wasn't easy last night, though."

"What happened?" Sandy asked.

"She was pretty agitated and difficult to talk to," Cynthia explained, "you know, angry about being here. She wouldn't go to sleep but just kept pacing up and down the hallway. She was kind of mumbling to herself, and if anyone spoke to her, she would shout, 'No! I am not going to answer any of your damn questions right now! Leave me the hell alone!'"

"Did she eventually calm down?" Sandy wondered.

"Yeah, after a Haldol and Ativan cocktail. She finally sat in one of the rocking chairs and was quiet, but I don't think she slept. She just rocked and rocked in the chair. And this morning so far, she has refused breakfast, refused to take a shower, and said she wouldn't participate in the group activities. So she's all yours now, Sandy!" Cynthia picked up her purse and started toward the door. "See you tomorrow!"

This all sounds pretty typical, Sandy thought. *No one is happy about being dragged in by the police in the middle of the night. But she does sound pretty agitated.*

INTERVIEWING LUCY

"Lucy, tell me about where you were living before you came here," Sandy prompted gently after they exchanged some initial small talk.

"At my daughter's," Lucy began softly. "When can I go back there?"

"I'll need to speak to her and see if she will let you go back," Sandy responded. Relatives were often hesitant to take back their family members after a conflict, so Sandy would not assume that returning Lucy to her daughter's house was a viable plan until she spoke to the daughter.

"She will," Lucy assured.

"Well, you might be right. But if she doesn't, where else would you like to go?" As a discharge planner, Sandy knew she needed to begin thinking about placement now.

"Just take me to my car." Lucy's voice was so even, almost emotionless, that Sandy couldn't determine what she thought of this option.

"I don't know, Lucy. Your car is more than a hundred miles away in Choctaw County. Let's talk first about what to do while you are here."

"I don't need a hospital. I just need to get out of here!" Lucy raised her voice and fidgeted in her chair. "I don't need to answer any questions, I just need my car! You don't have any right to keep it from me!"

"Lucy," Sandy responded, "I can imagine that you are feeling upset, and I want to help you get to your car. Let's talk a minute about it."

"Shut up, I don't want to talk to you." Lucy rose out of her chair and began pacing around the room. "You have no right to keep me here."

"I know you don't want to be here," Sandy responded. "But it will help me get you out of here if you can tell me a bit about what's going on."

"Nothing is going on. I just want to get back to my car and back to my daughter's house. She was mad at me, but it will be okay. I've lived there some over the years, and she'll let me come back."

"Okay," Sandy said. "Maybe we can give your daughter a call. Have you ever been in a place like this hospital before?"

"I am not crazy, and I have never been somewhere like this. This is a prison. Go ahead, call my daughter! Tell her to come get me out of here now."

TRACY SAYS NO

Lucy signed release forms for Sandy to call her daughter, Tracy Bryson. Tracy lived in Idabel, Oklahoma, with her husband, two sons, and two stepchildren. Sandy caught her up on how Lucy had arrived at their unit.

"Does your mom have a history of mental illness?" Sandy asked.

"Yeah," Tracy answered. "She's bipolar. She does okay for a while, and it's okay with her staying here, but then she loses it. She has never really had a place on her own. She was staying here, but then I kicked her out. She lives in her car a lot of the time."

"She's telling me that she wants to come back to live with you after she's released. Is that going to work?"

"No, she can't come back here," Tracy stated flatly. "She's done too much, and I just can't put my family through that again. She gets so mad, and she tears up my house. She will go days without sleeping, and she'll get more and more angry about everything. This last time she was in the kitchen, and I told her that I needed to get to the sink to get a glass, and she took out a knife and said she would kill me if I got any closer to her. Then she threw some plates on the floor and threw my skillet through the window. The kids were around, and they saw all that. Everyone's afraid of her. She doesn't ever help with any of the chores or the bills, and I'm just done. I can't do this anymore."

"Are there other family members that might want to be involved with helping her?" Sandy asked. "What do you think is the best option for her, Tracy?"

"Everyone else is either dead or done with her. I don't want to see her suffer, but there's got to be some kind of a place for her. I love my mom, and I want to help her," Tracy's voice suddenly became quieter, "I really do, but she just can't come back." She sounded sad, as if she might be crying. "It has always been like this: she's here, and then she's not. We have tried to get her to see a doctor, and she just won't do it for long enough for it to ever help her. I can't do this to the rest of my family anymore. I just can't. I told my husband that if she comes back, we'll call the police and have her taken off the property. I hate to do that, but I just can't do this anymore. I'm sorry."

As Sandy hung up, she felt defeated and sad. It must be an awful feeling on both sides to have such difficulty with a parent. But it sure didn't help Sandy figure out what to do.

SEVENTY-TWO HOURS AND COUNTING

Because Lucy was an admitted on an emergency detention, the unit had seventy-two hours to assess her and provide a petition to the court indicating its conclusions and recommending either release or further detention for treatment. The judge would then decide whether the hospital could continue to detain Lucy against her will.

But the hearing had to take place in the county where the complaint originated, so this time Sandy sent the petition for continued detention as well as the records of the mental health evaluation to Choctaw County. The Choctaw County court clerk would then process the records. The court did not require that anyone from the unit be present during the proceedings, so Sandy wrote the petition immediately following her interview with Lucy (see "Exhibit A" at the end of this case) and faxed the records to the court clerk.

Several hours later Marjorie walked into her office with the faxed report from the court clerk. "The judge didn't continue the order," Marjorie said.

"Why not?" Sandy was shocked and immediately felt a sense of panic. "I wrote a good report! She can't go yet. Where is she going to go?"

"Well," Marjorie said, "the judge said she seemed stable enough despite the report that she wasn't participating in treatment. She isn't threatening to do anything to anybody right now, so she didn't come off as being a current threat."

Sandy opened the chart and scanned her report, hoping to find an answer. The courts tended to like a one-page letter, and Sandy always followed the same format. *This report should have been enough*, she thought.

"Well," Sandy said, "I'll call Adult Protective Services then. I'll see if they will assume guardianship of Lucy, and then they can help her get housed and find outpatient treatment."

"See what you can do, Sandy, but we have just twelve hours until we have to release her." Marjorie turned and left Sandy's office.

PLAN B: ADULT PROTECTIVE SERVICES

Sandy knew the Adult Protective Services (APS) workers well and was always pleased to live in a county where they were so responsive. When she called, she asked for Renee Colbert. She had always had good luck with Renee's willingness to assess patients and act quickly.

"Great to hear from you, Sandy," Renee said. "What can we do for you?"

Sandy summarized the whole story of Lucy, her symptoms, and the judge's disregard of Sandy recommendation to continue the emergency detention. "It is so frustrating, Renee, because we know this woman shouldn't be out on her own with no place to go. But apparently the Choctaw County judge thinks he knows better than we do."

Renee was quiet for a moment. "I get that you are frustrated, but here's the problem. If the court has already ruled that she isn't a danger to herself or anyone else, there isn't a lot that APS can do. If we go in and try to say we need guardianship because she really is dangerous, it has already been legally determined that she is not. If she had never gone through your unit and the continuance hearing, we might be able to do something, but for now APS can't really help you."

"You have got to be kidding me!" Taken aback, Sandy asked, "What am I going to do now?"

PLAN C: THE CHOCTAW NATION

After Sandy ended her conversation with Renee, she tried to think of another option. She'd call the Choctaw Nation. Lucy was Native American, and Sandy had helped other patients find affordable and safe housing through the services provided by the Choctaw Nation. The nation provided many services, including social services and employment counseling, so it could probably provide Lucy with numerous opportunities to have a better quality of life. It was worth a shot.

She called the Choctaw Nation Housing Department and spoke to Amanda Wright. She had worked with Amanda on a previous case and knew that Amanda was familiar with the hospital. Again, she summarized Lucy's situation.

"Sure," Amanda said, "sounds like she'd qualify. You can download the application from our website and give it to her, and we'll do our best to make a match. It might be a few days until we can have something ready for her, but we'll do our best to speed it up."

Sandy was relieved. Lucy might have a chance of housing after all! She didn't know how either she or Amanda would complete the process in just twelve hours, but she knew they were willing to try. She couldn't wait to tell Lucy about this good option.

THE NEXT STEP

Sandy located Lucy in the TV room and sat down across from her. Lucy was slumped in her chair, looking at the floor. *After that first day of being so angry, she has become really withdrawn*, Sandy thought. *She has just been flat and silent.*

"Lucy, great news," Sandy began. "We're going to discharge you soon. Have you given any more thought to where you would like to go?"

"To my daughter's." Lucy's tone was still flat, and her voice quiet.

"Lucy," Sandy said calmly, "remember, we told you we spoke with her, and she said no. You can't go back there."

"She says stuff like that, but she'll let me. Just get me back there, and it will be okay."

"She said she'd call the police. She really was clear; you can't stay with her anymore." Lucy's daughter had been clear. She would not accept Lucy back into her home. Lucy had nowhere else she wanted to go and no one to manage her care.

"Lucy," Sandy said, "your daughter said you couldn't come back this time."

"It will be fine," Lucy spoke evenly. "Just take me to my car, and I'll get there myself then."

"Lucy, your car really isn't a safe place for you right now." Sandy felt herself getting frustrated. *Taking someone to a broken-down car is not an appropriate discharge plan!* "It's summer, and it's hot out. It's too hot to be in a closed-up car. And your car isn't working. I've spoken to the Choctaw Nation, and there are options to find you housing with them. We could find you a place where you would be safe and comfortable." Sandy feared she was starting to plead.

"That's okay, I don't need housing. I just like it with my daughter. And if she doesn't want me, it's okay in the car. I'll figure it out, I've done it before."

That is not going to work, Sandy thought. *That is not a discharge plan in your best interests! Dropping off an elderly woman with a mental illness at her broken down car is NOT what I consider an appropriate discharge plan! But I have to discharge her soon! What am I going to do with her?*

EXHIBIT A

Durant Regional Health Services

Geriatric Psychiatric Services Unit
1760 East Elm Street
Durant, OK 74701

July 29, 2008

To Whom It May Concern:

Lucy Haskins (DOB 11-10-44) is a 63-year-old Native American female admitted to the Geriatric Psychiatric Services Unit on 7-28-08. She was brought to the unit by the Sheriff's Department of Choctaw County. At the time of referral, she had been found wandering on the highway and threw rocks at the deputies as they attempted to apprehend her. She was previously living with her daughter and is reported to have threatened the daughter with a knife, stating, "I will kill you if you come closer to me."

She then threw objects through a window and kicked a hole in the wall.

Her daughter reports that she is fearful of her mother and is refusing to allow her to return to the home. There are children in the home, and the daughter feels the children are not safe around Ms. Haskins. The daughter reports that Ms. Haskins has a history of bipolar disorder and has only sporadically been treated. At the time of admission, Ms. Haskins was taking no medications for the treatment of this disorder.

Upon admission, Ms. Haskins had an agitated affect and has been noncompliant with mental health assessments. She has refused to answer questions and has appeared agitated and angry. She has demanded her release, stating, "Nothing is wrong with me." She has refused meals and showers and has refused to sleep. She has not engaged in group activities.

She did engage in the Mini Mental Status Exam this morning, where she scored 22/30, which indicates a low to moderate level of cognitive impairment, and the Geriatric Depression Scale, where she scored 15/30, which indicates a low to moderate level of depression. Based on the information gathered in initial assessments of Ms. Haskins, we believe| she would benefit from continued assessment, including a complete diagnostic assessment, and treatment to stabilize her mood and behaviors. We request that she remain on the unit and that the emergency order of detention be continued. We believe that if released, she will be unable to care for herself and could be a potential danger to herself or to others. Based on her behaviors, we respectfully request that she be excused from her court appearance as we believe this could further agitate her condition.

Sincerely,

Jodie Hamilton, MD
Geriatric Psychiatrist

Marjorie Adams, LCSW
Social Work Supervisor

Sandy DeLoach, MSW
Discharge Planner

2

GAY-FOR-PAY

Lori D. Franklin

The Proud Youth teen group was scheduled to meet in a few minutes in a discreet group room at the far end of the second floor of the building. Max, Marcus, Stacy, Nikki, and Dalton were gathered in the lobby of Wichita Center for Families, waiting to be led back. But their group leader, MSW student Alicia Hall, was still in her office, waiting until the last minute.

As she looked back through her group notes from the previous week, Alicia thought, *The kids deserve a response from me, but I still don't know what to do about what they're saying in group! How am I supposed to react professionally to these stories of wild*

Development of this decision case was supported in part by the University of Oklahoma School of Social Work. It was prepared solely to provide material for class discussion and not to suggest either effective or ineffective handling of the situation depicted. Although the case is based on field research regarding an actual situation, names and certain facts may have been disguised to protect confidentiality. The author thanks the anonymous case reporter for cooperation in making this account available for the benefit of social work students and instructors.

drag shows, kids cutting themselves, and all the other stuff they're
telling me happens at another agency? Should I be doing something
about it?

GAY IN WICHITA

Wichita, Kansas, was a midsize city with beautiful parks and museums, running trails, a farmer's market, and Wichita State University. But it struggled in its acceptance of lesbian, gay, bisexual, and transgender (LGBT) people. Living in Kansas, as in much of the Midwest, brought with it a strong assumption of heterosexuality from the general public and an often vicious opposition to same-sex relationships. Almost 70 percent of Kansas voters had voted for the constitutional amendment to ban same-sex marriage in 2005.

The community had very few services for the LGBT population. There was an agency that provided HIV/AIDS advocacy and case management, and Kansas Pride operated a small office, staffed mostly with volunteers. Kansas Pride provided some social events, classes, and support groups that were usually poorly attended and usually for adults. Wichita's Annual Pride Festival often had more than one thousand attendees, proving there were LGBT people in the area, but it inevitably drew protestors. Wichita was a short drive from Topeka, home of the most famous of gay bashers, Fred Phelps, whose followers always attended the Pride festivities with protest signs with messages such as "Fag sin = 9-11" and "You're going to hell."

There were also very few services for LGBT youth. Two agencies identified themselves as serving this vulnerable population. Wichita Center for Families was a large agency that had a reputation for being "LGBT affirmative." Rainbow Alliance for Youth was the only agency designed specifically to serve LGBT youth.

WICHITA CENTER FOR FAMILIES

Wichita Center for Families (WCF) provided a large variety of services for at-risk families and youth. Philosophically, the agency promoted family collaboration, was strength-based, and provided an environment that acknowledged and appreciated diversity. The agency provided on-site emergency services at the Kansas State Department of Human Services (KSDHS) youth shelter and a twenty-four-hour hotline for youth in crisis. Family counselors saw clients in the office but also provided services on-site in the schools. WCF also worked in collaboration with the Office of Probation and Parole to provide case management and counseling to youth involved with the justice system.

Among its services for youth, WCF had several initiatives specifically for LGBT youth as well as those questioning their sexual orientation. It worked in collaboration with the KSDHS to identify youth who were in need of LGBT-affirmative services. One program focused especially on homeless youth, and for several years WCF had provided a "coming out" support group.

WCF had also recently implemented an employment nondiscrimination policy to protect LGBT employees. That was unusual in the area, but the agency director felt strongly that it was an important way to show the agency was committed to doing what was right for the LGBT community.

RAINBOW ALLIANCE FOR YOUTH

The Rainbow Alliance for Youth (RAY) was a grassroots organization created by a male couple who shared great concern for LGBT youth. Their stated mission was to "promote the physical, mental, emotional, spiritual, and social well-being of sexual minority youth so that they can openly and safely explore and affirm their identities." But RAY was not just for LGBT youth. It welcomed youth who were questioning their sexual identities as well as friends of LGBT youth. It provided social opportunities on Saturday nights, which were often dances and drag shows featuring the youth. These events sometimes required a small cover charge, but the money was used to operate the agency. RAY also offered social opportunities on Wednesday nights, usually a dinner followed by discussions and supportive small-group activities.

ALICIA HALL

Alicia Hall was a petite white woman and had just turned twenty-five, although people often assumed her to be younger than that. She loved long-distance running and cooking healthy foods and was an avid fiction reader. She usually experienced surprise from others when they found out that she had a girlfriend instead of a boyfriend.

When Alicia entered the Wichita State University MSW program, she had two years of bachelor's level case management experience with adults with mental illnesses. Because her memories of growing up as a gay youth in Wichita were recent, she also had a passion for working with the LGBT community. Although Alicia had lived in the region most of her life and thought of it as her home, she had often felt confused and unwelcome in the difficult climate there. She didn't hide being a lesbian, but she didn't speak openly without first having a feel for the social context. She knew she had good boundaries about when and how to discuss her own sexual identity with clients and coworkers.

FIRST IMPRESSIONS

Alicia had heard about RAY while growing up in the area but had never been there. But early in the MSW program, a fellow student, Melanie Shelton, offered to give her a tour. Melanie had been volunteering at RAY and wondered if Alicia might like to do so as well.

"Hey," Melanie said, "I'd like to show you around this place where I was volunteering. I'm too busy with school these days, so I quit, but I really think they could use someone like you with a bit more of a background in social services and all. They have good intentions, but there's a lot of kind of strange stuff that goes on there—you know, like smoking and all."

As the two women entered the unmarked building, Alicia first noticed the black walls and the large open room with a stage at the front. *This looks like a club*, she thought. Noticing some office space with a couch that had a pillow and a blanket on it, she wondered, *Do people sleep here?* As she continued to look around, she saw that was about the extent of the space. There was a unisex bathroom with several stalls and another room with a closed door. Out the back door, Melanie pointed to a dumpster in the alley behind the building where the kids went to smoke. Alicia remembered that Melanie had mentioned previously that youth as young as twelve participated at RAY. Unsure of Melanie's impressions of the agency, Alicia kept her reservations to herself.

"What do they do here?" she asked.

"Well," Melanie explained, "the kids watch movies, hang out, and there are lots of drag shows. It's really a lot of fun for them, you know, to dress up and play around. Look at this!" Melanie opened the door to the last room and led Alicia inside. "It's the dressing room." There were wigs and dresses hanging on the walls, high-heeled shoes on the floor, and a countertop cluttered with makeup and cosmetic mirrors. There were full-length mirrors along the walls and a chair surrounded by hair-styling products. *Drag shows seem to be what this place is about*, Alicia thought. *I'm not sure if I like that or not.*

PRACTICUM PLACEMENT AT WCF

After completing her foundation practicum at her place of employment, Alicia wanted to work with LGBT youth during her concentration placement and knew that WCF had a good reputation. WCF was quite familiar with student social work placements from Wichita State. Several departments at the agency utilized bachelor's as well as master's level students. But Alicia's placement involved a new set of tasks for a student. She was supervised weekly by the clinical director of the agency, Pete Anderson, but she was housed within the "youth at risk outreach unit" and had a preceptor, Nancy Gerard, to supervise her day-to-day practice. With a master's in counseling, Nancy was a licensed professional counselor.

Alicia not only provided family counseling with LGBT youth and their families but also assumed leadership of a "coming out" support group for youth. She served as a liaison between the agency and the Gay–Straight Alliances (GSA) clubs in all of the Wichita public schools. She was especially excited about this part of the job, where she felt she could provide support and cultivate leadership among youth all over the city and help Wichita's fragmented and uncoordinated services for the LGBT community unite and work together for some of the city's most vulnerable youth.

The placement was very independent, but the supervision structure was designed to support Alicia's learning. When she saw families or youth in the office, she would have easy access to Nancy and the other therapists on site. But the group met in the evenings after Nancy had left for the day. And, of course, the outreach at the schools involved travel away from the facility without a supervisor nearby. But Pete made it clear that he would always be available by telephone if Alicia needed him.

FIRST DAYS IN THE PLACEMENT

On Alicia's first day at WCF, Nancy showed her around the office and introduced her to some of her new coworkers.

"Jack!" Nancy called loudly, trying to get the attention of the middle-aged white man at the end of the hall. He turned and walked toward Nancy and Alicia.

"I'd like you to meet our new MSW student," Nancy said. Alicia shook Jack's hand.

"Alicia will be working with the coming out group and the GSA project while she's here this semester," Nancy explained. "This is Jack McCormick, the Outreach Program director."

"It's nice to meet you," Alicia responded.

"I'm glad we'll have some fresh ideas in that group," Jack said. "It's been run by lots of folks. Most recently it was run by a fella who just shared too much of his personal stuff. He was talking about his dates and all, and it just turned into a chat instead of a group, you know? And then we had Kelly do it for a while, but she has other things to do."

"Thanks," Alicia said, "I'm looking forward to it."

"And who knows," Jack continued, "it might turn into a job for you when you're done. We've been looking to hire us a gay-for-pay for quite a while."

What? Alicia thought, alarmed. *Does he not know the origin of that term? Where on earth did that come from?*

"What do you mean?" she finally asked.

"Well, you know," Jack said, "a full-time gay person to really focus on the gay issues here in this agency."

"Oh," Alicia responded, "well, I look forward to working with you."

THE RAY OF HOPE

A few days into her placement, Alicia shadowed a family counselor as part of her orientation to the practices at WCF. Victor Clark had worked in the family-counseling program for more than a year and invited Alicia to watch him interview a new client. Alicia pulled a chair in from another room and sat facing the young woman, Sasha, and her mother.

Alicia followed along on her own copy of the intake paperwork while Victor interviewed Sasha and her mother. The paperwork asked for the client's sex (male or female) and orientation (heterosexual, lesbian, gay, or bisexual), and then there was a checkbox if the client was transgender. Alicia looked ahead and saw that later in the form the client was asked, "Is there anything related to your sexuality that you wish to discuss in counseling?" *Wow*, Alicia thought to herself. *I am not sure how I would ask those questions, especially since the kids will often have their parents in the room. If I were doing this, I might save some of those to the end and ask to speak to the child alone. I wonder what Victor will do with those.*

"Sasha," Victor asked hesitantly, "you are female, right?"

"Well, yeah," she answered. Her eyebrows lowered.

"And do you like boys or girls or both?" Victor continued.

"Girls," Sasha said slowly. She seemed uncomfortable to Alicia. Sasha, Alicia, and Victor glanced at Sasha's mom. Her facial expression seemed tense but didn't change as Sasha spoke.

Alicia noticed that Victor skipped the transgender question.

"Do you have a religious affiliation?" he asked.

"They are Southern Baptist," Sasha stated flatly, looking toward her mother.

Victor continued with questions, and Alicia listened intently. *I probably would have asked her to say more about her struggles with coming out as a lesbian in such a conservative religious family,* Alicia thought. *That seems important.*

Victor moved on to the mental health history portion of the assessment form.

"Have you ever had thoughts of suicide?" he asked.

"I guess sometimes I just thought things would be easier if I were dead. But I never really was going to do it." Sasha spoke more easily and shrugged her shoulders. "But whenever I've felt like that, the only people that really understood me were the guys at RAY. They really are the only people who seem to get what it's like to be a gay kid."

"I do not want her going to that place full of sinners anymore," Sasha's mother quickly interjected. "That is not what Jesus wanted for her life, and, plus, they are smoking and doing all sorts of stuff over there that is just not right."

"No one is ever going to understand someone like me," Sasha continued, "especially not my family." Looking at her mother, she added, "It's a place where they accept you like no one else in society ever will."

Alicia felt a strong empathy for Sasha and anxiety about the extent of the mother's resistance about her daughter's sexual orientation. She knew too well that there were parents in Kansas who could become violent with their children or kick them out of the house when they found out their children were gay.

PROUD YOUTH

A week into her placement Alicia met with Kelly Lander to discuss the group that Alicia would soon be leading herself. As Jack had mentioned, Kelly had been facilitating the group but did not want to continue. As the agency's health educator, she had focused more on health education and in the group had mostly discussed psychoeducational material on safe sex and HIV prevention. Alicia asked Kelly for a little background on the group members.

"Sure," Kelly said, opening the first chart on the stack. "Max is sixteen, biracial, white and African American and has been at the shelter about six months. He's in the job skills program here and does some janitorial stuff in the building for that." Alicia immediately wondered whether he was the friendly kid she had seen talking to the receptionist earlier that morning.

"Marcus is seventeen," Kelly continued, "African American, and came to the shelter after a string of failed foster placements. He's been with lots of foster families that have kicked him out for being gay. It's really sad. He just got out of the hospital after his most recent foster mother found him hanging in the garage. He was okay, but they said they couldn't keep him anymore, so now he's here at the shelter. I know he had one foster family who was Southern Baptist, and they tried to take him to one of those religious programs to try to 'cure' him before they gave up on the placement."

"That sounds awful," Alicia said. "Poor kid."

"Yeah," Kelly went on, "then there's Dalton, who is sixteen and white, kind of upper middle class and at some private school. His folks are going to family counseling with him, and that all seems to be going along okay."

"Then there's Stacy, who is seventeen, lives with her mom. Her folks got divorced when her dad came out. She gets into fights at school a lot and identifies as a lesbian, but I'm not really sure where she's at with her identity."

Alicia nodded and kept on listening.

"And finally, Nikki," Kelly said as she put the last chart on the stack. Alicia noticed the chart said "Nicholas." "Fifteen, white and Creek, transgender, run away from at least four different foster placements, and now refuses further placement. His mom drank and abused the kids, so Nikki was removed at age ten, and there are some older siblings who are now on their own. It never has really worked out, I guess, to place Nikki with one of them."

"So there you have it, Alicia," Kelly said. "There's your group! I am really glad you are here. I think it will really help these kids to have a leader with a social work background."

THE GROUP MEETS

In their first few sessions, Alicia quickly tried to revitalize the group and get it back on track as a support group with a psychoeducation component. She was bothered by the name of the group—LGBT

Support Group—and encouraged the kids to select a new name. They came up with "Proud Youth."

She soon implemented some activities in the group. For example, she asked the kids to draw questions out of a hat about their experiences of coming out; they played a trivia game about famous LGBT people; and they watched *Brokeback Mountain* and discussed it as a group. She divided the group meetings into a discussion activity section and a psychoeducation section with presentations about safe sex, relationship skills, self-esteem, and other issues that seemed relevant for group members.

The group members were actively engaged, seemed interested in the topics, and participated readily. They seemed to trust Alicia and talked freely about their lives. Sometimes before sessions, for example, they chattered about attending "parties" at RAY.

"They were so hot at that drag show the other night," she overheard Max saying.

"Yeah," Marcus answered, "did you see that dude taking those pills in the bathroom? Don't know what that shit was he was taking."

"I didn't see that," Max said, "but I saw that one emo girl with the red streaks in her hair in there cutting her arms up. Seems like the emos are multiplying over there. Then later she was out in the smoke hole making out with that new girl like nothing ever happened."

"I don't think they should play all that emo music," Stacy chimed in. "It just attracts them, and they show up there to do all that cutting and stuff. It's gross."

"Well, they aren't going to fit in anywhere else but RAY," Marcus responded. "Most of them are bi anyway, so RAY understands them."

Is RAY allowing this kind of stuff to happen? Alicia worried. *Are they encouraging it?* She knew a little about the "emo" culture and how difficult it was to treat someone who thought cutting themselves was not only cool, but an important way to express emotion. *But surely RAY is not allowing these kids to take pills and cut themselves without doing anything about it!*

She wasn't sure what to say to the kids because they were just talking among themselves outside of the group. It wasn't group time yet, so she wasn't sure how to intervene. But she could see that Max looked over at her and seemed to be waiting for her to say something.

As Alicia got used to her direct practice work with the youth at WCF, she began to move more into the GSA liaison part of her placement. She had an idea to create a conference for the leaders and members of local GSA clubs in the high schools. She started working with leaders of Kansas Pride, the agency that organized the events for the annual Pride Festival. Kansas Pride had undergone community criticism for its lack of attention to youth issues, so its organizers welcomed the opportunity to collaborate with Alicia. They were adamant, though, about not even attempting to collaborate with RAY.

"We have asked them before about their board of directors, and they won't even tell us the names of the members," Assistant Director Kiara Junger told Alicia. "We have asked about their policies, if there is anyone with any kind of credentials on their staff, and all of that. They will not even answer our questions. The last thing that Kansas Pride needs is any more conflict with RAY."

"Why doesn't anyone do something about them?" Alicia asked. "Isn't there somewhere to report them?"

"Well," Kiara said hesitantly. "I don't know what it would do to the gay community to have the stuff that goes on there exposed. It might just confirm so many stereotypes that we are always trying to overcome, you know?"

Alicia agreed not to attempt to collaborate with RAY on the conference. *I'm not sure what I can do as a student, anyway*, she thought. *This sounds like a rift that's been there for quite a while.*

Alicia began canvassing local high schools to hang posters about the conference and asking to talk to principals about encouraging their LGBT students to attend. She was quickly discouraged by the response. She felt unprepared for the looks from staff when she showed them her poster and asked if she could hang it up. She was told several times that she could not hang her poster and was asked to leave. She had principals tell her they were unavailable to meet with her or that there was no reason to meet because there were no gay children in their schools. *Maybe this wasn't the right placement for me*, Alicia thought. *I'm taking this rejection way too personally. I'm still too sensitive right now to serve gay clients in such a conservative community. But I have to see this practicum through at least. I just don't want to ruin my professional reputation before my career even starts!*

When the day of the conference rolled around, mostly adults showed up. The conference went well, with great speakers, a live band, and great food, but a very disappointing attendance. Even some youth that Alicia herself had talked to didn't show up.

The following Monday morning Alicia saw Max in the hallway outside her office space. He was mopping the floor, so she stepped out to talk to him.

"Max," she asked, "do you know why the kids from group didn't show up for the conference on Saturday?"

"RAY scheduled a party for that night. It was a special event, a drag show contest, and they elected Miss RAY that night." Max looked at the floor.

"Right, I thought RAY just did stuff on Saturday nights?" Alicia responded. "This was all on Saturday morning and afternoon, so couldn't they have gone to both things?"

"They pushed the start time to noon, just to make sure there was time for everyone to do their number." Max looked up at Alicia.

Great, she thought. *Music, food, and education will never be able to compete with wild parties.*

IS THIS GAY-FOR-PAY?

One afternoon for group Alicia began with an exercise, hoping to create more feelings of commonality among members. She had left the previous session feeling concerned that Stacy didn't fit in well with the other kids.

"If you could be a superhero, who would it be?" Alicia began.

"I don't know, I guess I'd just want to have the power to be liked by people for who I am and not have to hide myself," Marcus said. "I think I might be trans, but how do you know if you want to have a sex change? My DHS caseworker is really cool, and she was telling me she could help me start doing hormones and stuff if I wanted to. Since I had that bad suicide attempt and all last year, I probably could never even get anyone to do hormones for me."

"I don't know how you know, you just know," said Nikki. "It's good you go to RAY because they really understand all that. They can help you, you know, they really get it there. They have really been cool with helping me and showing me how to do my hair and makeup."

"Do you think we 'get it' here at WCF?" Alicia asked.

"Well," Nikki began. "When I first met my counselor here, he was like, 'Do you like boys, or do you like girls?' I mean, I'm a girl, so if I like boys, was he going to write down I was straight or what?"

"I didn't know what to say," Nikki continued. "Then he was like, 'Do you like chickens? I mean, boy, those feathers!' I didn't even know what he was talking about. I don't think I ever even answered his question because I really don't know if I like boys or girls. Was that like a joke, or what?"

"I would have just told him to shut up," Stacy responded. "What a moron." She slugged Nikki on the arm, friendly but too hard. Nikki shot her a dirty look.

"I mean, people have always said I seem like a girl, the way I act, and I'm just glad that RAY was there to help me figure out that stuff," Nikki said.

"Yeah," said Marcus, "they've helped me learn a lot about how to do my makeup and dress up and stuff. It's fun there. The other night, though, I tried to walk over there with my boobs on and my dress and high heels. It was several miles, and I got pretty lost. It's hard to find them in the dark."

"Wait a minute, Marcus," Alicia interrupted. "I didn't know that you were wanting to start dressing like a woman. You've never mentioned that before."

"Well, sure. You know, it's fun," Marcus responded. "The drag shows are fun, and we get tips. It's kind of a way to make a little money. And I mean they are so cool and all. I know there was that one guy whose parents kicked him out when they found out he was queer, and the guys at RAY just let him stay there so he'd be safe. That was great, you know, I mean it sure beats coming to a shelter."

"Was this late at night when you were out walking?" Alicia asked. "Were you supposed to be back at the shelter? Did you feel safe?"

"Yeah, it was all fine," Marcus answered.

"So it's pretty fun there at RAY?" Dalton asked. "Do you think I should go sometime? I mean, what do you think, Alicia?"

"It is cool there, but I don't go anymore," said Max. "I mean it's cool to go there to party and all, but I don't know. It just seems like . . . I don't know . . . "

"Well, I don't know either. What do you guys think?" It was the best response Alicia could think of at the moment. But she wondered, *What is going on over there at RAY?*

SEEKING SUPERVISION

The next morning Alicia went to see Pete. In luck, she found him in his office, and he had time to talk. As soon as she mentioned issues with the group, Pete recommended asking Kelly to come join them. He thought that as a former group facilitator who knew the kids she could offer some insight. Alicia summarized her concerns about activities going on at RAY.

"How am I supposed to react when they say this stuff in group?" she asked. "I mean, I don't want to tell them I think they shouldn't go there because they like it so much; I'm afraid they'll just go there and never come back here again for legitimate services. And we could just forget about ever collaborating with RAY or really getting referrals from any kids in need that show up there."

"Well," Pete said, "you're right that we don't want to burn bridges and tell the kids not to go there. Maybe you could just talk about safety more generally and try to get them to talk about safety issues with each other. See what they think of RAY, like you started doing. As the group leader, you don't want to come in and say that RAY is bad, but maybe you can help them figure out for themselves what they think."

"That's what I want to do," Alicia said. "I want to figure out how to use the group process to help them evaluate it for themselves. I just don't know how to respond in a way that's professional."

"No way," Kelly said. "Don't talk about RAY in your group at all. Just change the subject if they bring it up. We already have a turf war here. Just stay away from that subject."

"Well," Pete responded. "I get what you're saying, Kelly, and I think Alicia needs to think about that." Then, turning back to Alicia, "I still think there's therapeutic value to this, and you can use it to facilitate some important discussions with the kids. Just try it in your group next time. You can do this!"

"Thanks, Pete," Alicia responded hesitantly.

ONE WEEK LATER

As Alicia prepared for group, she looked back through her notes from the previous week and remembered Pete's encouragement. *The kids deserve a response from me, but I still don't know what to do about what they're saying in group! How am I supposed to react professionally to these stories of wild drag shows, kids cutting themselves, and all the other stuff these kids are telling me happens at RAY?*

Great, Alicia fretted, *I've thought about this a lot but still don't know exactly what to say! How am I going to use our time in group today? Do I have an obligation to do anything about what they say? If so, what?*

3

BUT SOMEONE COULD DIE!

Karen A. Gray and Anna Woodham

Because social worker Lilya Robles feared lives were in danger, she had not hesitated to make a late-night call to her supervisor, Frances Malone. Although Frances was often blunt and sometimes insensitive, her response to Lilya's request for direction still stung. "Lilya," Frances said, "for almost a year now we've talked about how you wear your heart on your sleeve and how you get too involved. You do not need to get involved in this. You need to mind your own business. You're out of your league. Just leave it alone. You're overreacting. Now, good night."

Lilya hung up, no less panicked than before the call. *Is she right? Am I overreacting? I know I can get too involved with my clients. But*

Development of this decision case was supported in part by the University of Oklahoma School of Social Work. It was prepared solely to provide material for class discussion and not to suggest either effective or ineffective handling of the situation depicted. Although the case is based on field research regarding an actual situation, names and certain facts may have been disguised to protect confidentiality. The author thanks the anonymous case reporter for cooperation in making this account available for the benefit of social work students and instructors.

*Annie might be in danger. What if George tries to kill someone?! What
if I do nothing and people die?!*

TULSA DOMESTIC VIOLENCE INTERVENTION SERVICES

Domestic Violence Intervention Services (DVIS) in Tulsa, Oklahoma,
had provided services for survivors of domestic violence in Tulsa and
Tulsa County since 1976. By 2001, its services included shelters, counseling for survivors and perpetrators, children's programs, advocacy,
public education, and a new permanent-housing program.

The permanent-housing program housed five families and was supported by local government funding. The program provided housing
for domestic violence survivors who were homeless because of violence
and disabilities.

Participants in the permanent-housing program received case management and individual and group counseling as a requirement of the
program and paid some portion of rent based on a sliding scale. As
part of agency policy, staff members were not to transport clients.
These requirements were designed to help participants work toward
the goal of self-sufficiency.

At DVIS, there were divergent beliefs about how to help survivors.
Some staff members thought it was important to help clients in any
way possible, even if it meant "doing for" instead of "doing with,"
whereas others thought that approach was too similar to perpetrators'
controlling behavior. Most of the administrators thought it was important to let clients make mistakes; at least they were making their own
decisions instead of obeying their abuser. But most of the frontline
staff members found this practice too difficult.

DVIS STAFF

Lilya Robles was a young, second-generation Puerto Rican who had
grown up in New York City. She was bilingual, bright, and energetic
and spoke at a fast pace. Friendly and kind, she quickly bonded with
people and was well liked. She wanted to work in a medical setting

because she had enjoyed her internship at the University of Oklahoma Medical Center. However, there were no positions available in medical social work, so she accepted a position as a counselor with DVIS, her first job since receiving her master's in social work. In 2002, six months after she began working at DVIS, she had finished developing the new permanent-housing program policies, procedures, and forms and was promoted to "assistant coordinator" of that program.

Lilya had not planned on working with domestic violence survivors because of events in her own life. Lilya's mother had been a survivor of domestic violence, and Lilya debated with herself whether to take the job at DVIS. *I've seen it all my life. I never wanted to work with that population. I saw my mom get beat up. I saw my aunts get beat up. Sometimes Mom would go back to him, and I couldn't understand why she would choose him over me.*

Soon after accepting the position, she reflected on her own history and her decision to accept the job. *I didn't realize that I'm a domestic violence victim until I started working here. I didn't think it was domestic violence because I was sixteen and seventeen, and now I'm a woman, and I can say no. I didn't know that his choking me back then was domestic violence.* The first time Lilya realized that she was herself a domestic violence victim, she cried the whole night. But she concluded the next day, *Working with victims of domestic violence—it could be just too close to home. . . . I'll give DVIS a year.*

Because Lilya's internships were in short-term and crisis settings, she had not experienced working with clients in long-term relationships. For her, the supportive housing program "was really different. Going into their homes, learning about their personal life." Although Lilya understood DVIS administration's view on allowing clients to make mistakes and bad choices, she wasn't sure she wanted to emulate this.

Lilya's immediate supervisor, Francis Malone, was the coordinator of several programs at DVIS. Francis had a master's degree in education and had previously worked as a high school principal. She was white and in her late fifties. With her short hair, button-down shirts, masculine pants, and chain smoking, she looked older. She had family members who were survivors of domestic violence and was very dedicated to helping survivors. Frances was too busy to be a micromanager, and her pragmatic approach to work sometimes bordered on gruff. She believed it was sometimes important, as she said, to let a client "fall on her face" because rescuing a client was too much like the control an abuser had over his victim.

Lilya often spoke to Frances about her own responses to her clients, looking for guidance and an empathetic listener. To Lilya, it seemed that Frances's responses usually lacked warmth or understanding. At one point, Frances told Lilya, "You need to build some tough skin. Stop letting things into your heart."

Another colleague, Beverly Harris, had worked at DVIS as a counselor for some twenty years. Beverly had no formal education or training but believed she was qualified, as she said, "by the school of hard knocks." She was white and middle-aged.

REBECCA JOHNSON

Rebecca Johnson, a thirty-six-year-old white female, had been a client at DVIS off and on for many years. She had suffered a closed head injury after an automobile accident when she was five years old, which affected her ability to process information and impaired her relationships with others. In addition to domestic violence, this disability made it difficult for the staff to find a housing placement for Rebecca.

Rebecca was married to George, her second husband, who was mentally and physically abusive. They had three children together. Rebecca also had two older children with her first husband, but she had relinquished parental rights to them.

Rebecca had worked with Beverly exclusively for years. Rebecca always asked for Beverly. It didn't matter what Beverly's job position was, Beverly would work with her.

"I THINK WE CAN REALLY HELP HER"

Not long after Lilya started with the DVIS and the permanent-housing program, Beverly knocked on Lilya's door and sat down in her office.

"Lilya," Beverly began, "Rebecca Johnson should be the first client in the permanent-housing program. She is the reason Frances applied for the Housing and Urban Development grant—so we could create this program for her and clients like her. I've been working with her on and off for more than seven years. I'm her only counselor because she trusts me. So even though she hasn't always technically been in whatever program I'm working in, I always see her. She's been a victim for most of her life, including being a victim of CPS in my opinion. I think she should get her kids back."

"Please," Lilya responded, "tell more about her."

Beverly quickly got to the point, "She came to the agency after CPS got involved with her kids. Her abusive husband, George, had pointed a gun at their oldest daughter's head and threatened to kill her. He didn't shoot her and shot the stove instead."

Lilya closed her eyes and took a deep breath, "What did Rebecca do then?"

"Rebecca was scared and pled for help from members of her Parent's Anonymous group, who called CPS. When CPS took temporary custody of the children, Rebecca decided she was not going to be with him anymore, and George moved to a house outside of Tulsa. CPS and the police could never find George, so he was never arrested. CPS returned the children to Rebecca on the condition that she receives counseling from DVIS, and I was her assigned counselor. Rebecca had been in and out of DVIS when she had her first child with George. She didn't do well in group because of her traumatic brain injury, and she didn't like going to TBI support groups outside DVIS because she thought she wasn't as bad off as the other members. She didn't follow through with individual sessions on campus, so we did most of our work at outreach visits.

"Rebecca and her girls lived in an apartment, and they received a lot of assistance from several agencies besides DVIS. Many people were involved in helping her care for herself and her children, including a home care aide. In spite of the amount of assistance, Rebecca was still not able to maintain a clean household for the children.

"Six months after George moved out, the CPS worker discovered that Rebecca was pregnant again and that George was the father. According to the case plan, George was not allowed near the children because he was the abuser. After questioning, Rebecca eventually blurted out, 'We had sex outside, not in the apartment near the kids!' Of course, that meant no one was watching the children inside, so CPS put the children in a foster home.

"As Rebecca's due date for her fifth child approached, she disappeared. We had no idea what happened to her until her CPS worker from Tulsa and another worker from New Mexico found her living in New Mexico."

"What happened to her," Lilya leaned forward, "and how did they find her?"

"It turns out," Beverly said, "that she and George decided to have their baby and live in Mexico—don't ask me what they were thinking. They decided to just forget about the two girls and focus on the new baby. Rebecca gave birth in a Mexican hospital, but she and George couldn't pay for the care, and the hospital wouldn't release the baby. A missionary family provided money to get the baby out of the hospital and then moved Rebecca and the baby to New Mexico and paid for one month's rent. George went back to Tulsa because there were things he needed to 'straighten out' in Oklahoma first. Then he was supposed to meet Rebecca back in New Mexico.

"For two weeks, Rebecca didn't hear from George. This is when the CPS worker from New Mexico and Rebecca's CPS worker from Tulsa knocked on her door. Rebecca let them inside, and they asked to see the baby.

"According to their case notes, Rebecca led them to the pallet on the floor where he was sleeping. He lay on blankets that had not been washed, surrounded by several dirty diapers. His skin was a jaundiced, pale yellow color, and he looked malnourished."

Lilya interrupted, "Was he born sick?"

"No, Rebecca had not been producing breast milk, and she had run out of money to buy formula. Rebecca's caseworker had to take this baby into custody, too.

"The CPS worker said Rebecca was distraught and couldn't understand why she and George couldn't raise their own children. She let Rebecca cry for a few moments, then told her again they had to take her son into custody and that they would try to place him with his sisters. She also told Rebecca they would have to reassess her visitation rights.

"She also had to tell her that George had been arrested in Tulsa for stealing money from his employer to pay for Mexico."

"Okay," Lilya said, making notes, "so that's how they found her."

"Yes," Beverly continued, "through the rest of the afternoon, the CPS workers and Rebecca developed a plan for Rebecca's move back to Tulsa. They made arrangements for her to rent a trailer at a reasonable rent, receive Supplemental Security Income, and contact the other agencies she was involved with, which included restarting counseling with me."

"Lilya," Beverly concluded earnestly, "I've worked with her a long time, and I think she's motivated now. With me counseling her and you working with her in the permanent-housing program, I think we can really help her."

"She has quite a story," Lilya responded. "Let's schedule an intake assessment to see if she's a fit for the permanent-housing program."

"THE FIRST TIME I MET HER, EVERYTHING WAS SO BEAUTIFUL AND WONDERFUL . . . "

The first time Lilya met Rebecca, five months after Lilya started working at DVIS, Beverly accompanied Lilya to Rebecca's trailer for the assessment. As Lilya pulled up to the trailer, she thought, *What a nasty, nasty trailer.* A brown film covered the outside of the once-white trailer. Weeds grew up the side of the trailer toward the roof line, which was no longer at straight angles. The wooden steps leading up to the door were no longer flush with the trailer and the first two steps showed signs of rot. The screen door was barely attached to the building, hanging on by only the top bracket. The windows were nailed shut, creating a fire hazard. Once inside, however, Lilya noted with surprise, *Everything's spotless, clean, beautiful. The dishes are put away, there's no clutter in the rooms, the floors have been recently vacuumed or mopped, and there's little dust to be found. Even the bathrooms are clean.*

Lilya and Rebecca discussed all five of her children, her closed head injury, verification of disability, and the type of apartment Rebecca needed. About her husband, George, Rebecca said, "He needs some help, but he's a very, very good man . . . he just gets mad sometimes, but that's his grandfather's fault."

Rebecca never called him her abuser, Lilya noted.

During the interview, Lilya became annoyed with Beverly because she interrupted the assessment, at times even speaking for Rebecca. Because Lilya was a new employee, and Beverly had worked with Rebecca for so long, Lilya hesitated to stop her.

Rebecca led Lilya through the trailer, showing Lilya the children's rooms. As Lilya surveyed the rooms, she realized, *Their toys are still in order . . . it looks as if the children just left last week.* For the past two years, there were clothes and Christmas toys that Rebecca had received from an agency for the children laid out neatly, still in packages ready for her children when they returned.

At the end of the visit, Lilya agreed to present Rebecca's case to the admissions committee. A week later the admissions committee agreed to admit Rebecca to the permanent-housing program.

"SOMETIMES SHE GETS LIKE THAT WHEN SHE'S WITH GEORGE . . . "

Lilya began to see Rebecca once a week for home visits and to transport her to supervised visits with her children every other week. The inside of the trailer that was once so clean and beautiful slowly began to resemble the outside of the trailer, until it smelled so bad that Lilya could no longer enter the trailer. Home visits became porch visits and restaurant visits. Rebecca had no money, so Lilya often took her to dinner and did their work during dinner. The visits usually lasted several hours because there were no other clients in the program yet, and Lilya had time to focus exclusively on Rebecca.

Rebecca's personal hygiene and health also declined slowly, contributing to the smell of the trailer. She told Lilya that she sometimes urinated on herself and would not change her pads often enough during her menstrual cycle even though Lilya bought sanitary pads for her. Because she was not taking regular showers, her hair got really greasy. When Lilya had first met Rebecca, she had exercised, gone to church, and attended her closed head injury group. When Lilya asked Rebecca why she had changed, Rebecca responded, "I'm miserable and depressed. I miss the kids."

Lilya spoke with Beverly about Rebecca's decline in functioning. "Rebecca has made a 180-degree turn since I met her. She told me she misses the kids, and I'm sure she does, but I think it's more. When I first met her, I'm sure she missed her kids then, too, but she was able to take care of the house and herself. She looked nice, and now she doesn't even shower. Plus, she was able to get together her paperwork for the program. Now she barely remembers when she has an appointment to go to."

"I've also noticed that she has appeared more depressed," Beverly replied. "She had been doing so well, losing weight, attending her closed head injury support group and Parent's Anonymous. She told me she had not been to any group or exercised in two weeks. As for completing her paperwork for the housing program and the clean house, I did most of it for her. And her hygiene . . . well, this is more the norm for Rebecca."

"You completed her paperwork and cleaned the trailer?!" Lilya asked, confused. She briefly recalled her orientation with Frances, who stressed that in the effort to help clients end the abuse cycle they should be allowed to try things, even if it meant they would "fall on their faces."

"Yes," Beverly replied. "I don't think she could have otherwise. But her recent depression and behavior . . . well, I'm sure she misses her kids, too, but in my experience her personal health declines when she is with George."

"With George?" Lilya questioned. "I hadn't thought about that." Lilya thought for a moment and then asked, "Do you know what George drives?"

"No," Beverly replied, "I'm not sure. Why?"

"There was a black-and-red motorcycle parked behind Rebecca's trailer last week. When I asked Rebecca whose it was, she told me it belonged to a neighbor, but now I'm not sure. Maybe its George's," Lilya pondered.

Later that day, as Lilya thought over her conversation with Beverly, she realized her first impression of Rebecca during the assessment interview was not accurate. She had assumed that Rebecca completed all her housing materials to enter the program, but now Beverly said she did not think Rebecca *could* have completed them on her own. Now it made sense to Lilya why Beverly had spoken for Rebecca so often during the assessment. Rebecca did not possess life skills as strong as Lilya originally believed but relied a great deal on others. Lilya was unsure of how much she should do for Rebecca but thought, *Well, she's in the program now, so let's give her a chance.*

After Lilya's conversation with Beverly, Lilya put more emphasis on discussing domestic violence issues (such as the "power and control wheel," financial abuse, setting boundaries) during her weekly meetings with Rebecca. It was required by the funder, but Lilya was also worried that Rebecca did not understand the real dangers that George presented. They reviewed Rebecca's goals weekly, but Rebecca continually stated as her main goal, "I want my kids back; I just want to be a mom." Lilya was not convinced that Rebecca understood what domestic violence was.

Three months later Rebecca moved out of the trailer and into a one-bedroom apartment provided by the program. Rebecca, one of her friends, Lilya, and Lilya's husband packed up Rebecca's belongings in heavy, black plastic bags and loaded them into the back of a van borrowed from the Salvation Army. Once Rebecca's belongings were in the new apartment, Lilya gave Rebecca a cleaning lesson. Lilya bought ammonia, vinegar, Mr. Clean——inexpensive things that Rebecca could buy herself in the future.

"I'm so happy to be in this new home, Lilya!" Rebecca beamed. "I'm going to take good care of it."

Despite Rebecca's intentions, the apartment did not stay clean for long and was filthy by the end of the month. Rebecca reunited with her dog, Max, who had been living with a friend for the past year. Lilya was surprised to see the dog because Rebecca had not discussed whether a dog could live in the apartment. But Lilya let her keep the dog, thinking it might make her feel better. The housing program paid for his shots and to get his teeth pulled.

SURPRISE INSPECTION

Once Rebecca moved in to her new apartment, CPS scheduled court hearings for three consecutive days to determine whether she could have custody of her and George's children.

The first day of the court hearings Lilya planned to do her monthly inspection of the apartment. When she arrived, Rebecca protested that there was not enough time to do an inspection, that they would be late for court. But Lilya pointed out that she had arrived early, so there was plenty of time. Lilya began her inspection in the kitchen and could see that the door to Rebecca's bedroom was open. When she and Rebecca moved into the living room and then walked back toward the bedroom, she noticed that Rebecca's bedroom door was now closed. Nervous that George might be in the house, Lilya said, "You're right. We don't want to be late, so we'd better go now."

Once in the car Lilya questioned Rebecca, "I know somebody is in the apartment. Who is it, and why is he or she there?"

"Oh, it's my friend," Rebecca replied, "um, it's my friend, the guy that works at Blockbuster, and, um, he came over this morning just to wish me luck for court."

"Well, why didn't you have him come out and introduce himself?" Lilya pushed.

"Because, you know, 'cause I didn't want him, you know, I didn't want him getting involved in my personal business."

"Then why was he in your bedroom if he's just coming to visit? Your bedroom is personal, so why was he there?"

"Oh, he's just watching TV."

Lilya knew the television set was in the living room, not the bedroom. But with little time left before the hearing, she dropped the topic and began to help Rebecca prepare emotionally for the court hearing.

COURT

For three days Lilya took Rebecca to court. The first day a psychiatrist testified that Rebecca would be unable to effectively parent children due to her head injury. The second day Rebecca lost custody of her son. The third day she lost custody of her two girls. The day Rebecca lost custody of the two girls, Lilya took her out to eat fish because Rebecca was feeling depressed and craving fish. Rebecca talked tearfully about the events over the past few days. The court had granted Rebecca three more visits with her children before they terminated her parental rights.

When Lilya asked Rebecca how she felt about the termination of her parental rights, Rebecca replied painfully, "I don't want to see my children anymore. I know I have three more visits, but after that I can't be their mother anymore. Those visits would just be too hard. This is all too hard, and I don't know what I'm going to do."

Lilya tried to empathize with Rebecca. She could imagine that losing her children would be very painful. But Lilya also felt the pain of her own childhood and thought, *Well, Rebecca, if you had just left George, you might still have your children!* However, Lilya recognized Rebecca's current despair and responded sympathetically, "What are some things that you can still do in your life that will help you be happy, even if you can't have your children with you?"

"I don't know! Nothing will make me happy . . . nothing. Lilya, I . . . I just want to die. I don't want to take my own life, but I want God to take my life!" Rebecca replied through her sobs.

"Okay," Lilya replied calmly, "you want to die, but you don't want to kill yourself. Is that correct?"

"Yeah, I guess that's right."

"Have you ever thought of a plan to kill yourself, Rebecca?" Lilya asked.

"No," Rebecca replied, calming down a little. "I don't want to kill myself, not really. It's just that this hurts so much."

"I can see that you are hurting right now," Lilya replied, "but try to talk to me about some things that you think can still be good about your life."

Rebecca took a deep breath and responded, "I could still have more kids, even if I can't keep the ones I have now."

"Yes, you are only thirty-six years old and still have a future that could include having more children."

"Although," Rebecca replied, "the CPS worker told me that if I ever have any more kids, I shouldn't tell anyone because they would have to take that baby away, too."

Lilya thought a moment and then responded, "Well, if you have another child, CPS may have to take the baby away. That is up to them to decide. Maybe you will have another baby, but I want you to think of good things in your life besides children before I talk to you tomorrow. And right now I want you to tell me that you are not going to kill yourself tonight when you go home."

"I don't like the idea of not having children again, but I will try to think of good things in my life. And I won't kill myself tonight."

"Okay, good," Lilya replied. "You have my home phone number. If you need to talk about anything, you can call me."

Rebecca called Lilya several times at Lilya's home often over the next two weeks just to talk.

"REBECCA JUST HAD A SEIZURE . . . "

Lilya had another client, Annie, who also lived in the same apartment complex as Rebecca. Lilya had introduced the two in the hope that they could help each other. Annie was also disabled and a survivor of domestic violence.

Annie called Lilya one day, panicked. "Lilya," Annie said in a rushed voice, "Rebecca just had a seizure. We're on our way to the hospital. You need to meet us there." Lilya hung up the phone and met Annie and Rebecca in the hospital an hour later.

When Lilya arrived at the emergency room, she could hardly stand to be there, the smell was so unbearable. Rebecca had urinated on herself during the seizure, and blood was all over her pants and the bed—due, Lilya assumed, to Rebecca's menstrual cycle. After a doctor went into Rebecca's room and did a pelvic exam, Lilya thought to herself, *What is he doing that for?* Lilya was in the hospital for five hours until Rebecca was discharged. Then Lilya drove Rebecca and Annie back to the apartment complex. Lilya put towels on the seat of her new car for Rebecca to sit on so that Rebecca wouldn't soil the fabric. They drove home with the windows down so that Lilya wouldn't gag.

When the three returned to Rebecca's apartment, Lilya told Annie, "You and I need to talk in your apartment." Annie had avoided her most recent inspection, and Lilya needed to address the issue with her.

"No, Lilya, you cannot talk to her now. I need to talk to her," Rebecca spoke up adamantly.

Lilya was tired but tried to reassure Rebecca, "You can talk with her later. We're not going to talk about you; we're going to talk about something else. Then I need to go home."

Lilya and Annie stepped into Annie's apartment. Lilya suspected that Annie sensed this conversation was about Annie's failure to uphold her end of the contract because she immediately redirected Lilya's attention: "Lilya, I have to talk to you. Rebecca is pregnant."

Lilya sighed heavily and told Annie, "Thank you for that information," then talked with Annie about her missed inspections. As Lilya left Annie's apartment, she thought, *The baby's father is probably the guy from Blockbuster. I'm too tired to talk to her right now about the pregnancy. I'll talk to her tomorrow.*

LATER THAT NIGHT

At 9:30 PM, Annie called Lilya for the second time that day. This time she sounded frightened.

"Lilya, you need to be very careful. George is in that apartment. When she had her seizure, and I yelled for someone to help me, a man immediately showed up. I thought he was a neighbor, and then the ambulance came. After you left my apartment this afternoon, I went back to Rebecca's apartment to see how she was doing. While I was there, a guy knocked on the door, and Rebecca let him in, and he had a black motorcycle helmet on. When he took the helmet off, I was like, 'Hey, you're the neighbor!' Then they both laughed, and Rebecca said, 'I need to tell you something. This is not the neighbor. This is my husband, George. He's been living here for a while, and I'm pregnant!' As we kept talking, they told me how mad George is at CPS. He said he wants to kill everybody: the judge, the CPS worker, and the foster parents. He is so mad at CPS for taking away his children! He says he's going to get all their addresses and go to their houses and shoot them. He's really mad, and he really means it!"

Lilya was silent for a moment, absorbing all Annie's information. She took a deep breath. "Annie, you need to be careful because now he's told you he has these intentions. Do you feel like you're safe there?"

"He knows where I live, Lilya, I'm scared."

"Okay," Lilya said quickly and decisively, "stay right there. I'm going to call my supervisor."

Lilya waited anxiously while the phone rang at Frances's house. When Frances answered, Lilya relayed the details of the day and the recent phone call: Rebecca's abuser was living with her, and he wanted to kill the judge, the CPS worker, and the foster parents.

"Frances, I think Annie needs to go into a shelter, for tonight at least. I'll pick her up and take her. I'm scared for her . . . this guy is crazy. I mean, he beats Rebecca and almost shot his daughter. I think he's capable of anything."

Frances was silent for a moment and then replied, "Lilya, for almost a year now, we've talked about how you wear your heart on your sleeve and how you get too involved. You do not need to get involved in this. You need to mind your own business. You're out of your league. Just leave it alone. You're overreacting. Now, good night."

· Lilya slowly hung up the phone, feeling no less panicked than before the call. *Is she right? Am I overreacting? I know I can get too involved with my clients. But Annie might be in danger. What if George tries to kill someone? Frances said to drop it . . . but what if I do nothing and people die?*

4

BELIEVING WOMEN

Gecole Harley and Terry A. Wolfer

In 2006, Lindsey Rickard, assistant director of the Victim Advocate Program for Florida State University, was sitting in a dorm room on Sunday afternoon. She was comforting Rachel Conway, a sexual assault survivor, as Jan Taylor, a university police investigator, took Rachel's statement. Rachel sat nearly motionless on her bed as she told Jan that she reported the attack to university police immediately.

"But the officer just came and laughed. He just laughed," Rachel said with a haunted look in her eyes.

What! Lindsey thought. *We have worked so hard to educate officers about client treatment. They're always so great. How can there still be officers who just don't get it?*

Development of this decision case was supported in part by the University of South Carolina College of Social Work. It was prepared solely to provide material for class discussion and not to suggest either effective or ineffective handling of the situation depicted. Although the case is based on field research regarding an actual situation, names and certain facts may have been disguised to protect confidentiality. The authors thank the anonymous case reporter for cooperation in making this account available for the benefit of social work students and instructors.

FLORIDA STATE UNIVERSITY

Tallahassee, Florida, home to Florida State University (FSU), was closer to Atlanta than to Miami geographically and culturally. In 2000, Tallahassee had a population of more than 150,000, with a racial/ethnic mix of 60.4 percent white, 34.2 percent black, 2.4 percent Asian, and 4.2 percent Hispanic or Latino. The Tallahassee area boasted the largest concentration of original plantations in the United States, but overall the area was a pleasant blend of old and new architecture, old and new customs, and old and new people.

In 1856, in response to the Florida legislature's desire to create two institutions of learning, Francis Eppes, the grandson of President Thomas Jefferson and the mayor of Tallahassee, offered the legislature the buildings and grounds owned by a boy's school. The legislature accepted, and FSU was conceived. From modest beginnings, FSU had developed to educate nearly forty thousand students from the baccalaureate through the doctoral level with fully accredited programs in law and medicine. Like other university campuses, FSU had its share of crimes. In 2004, FSU police officially received ten reports for forcible sex offences, six robberies, six aggravated assaults, fifty burglaries, three incidents of arson, and thirty motor vehicle thefts.

THE VICTIM ADVOCATE PROGRAM

The FSU Victim Advocate Program functioned under the auspices of the Dean of Students Department. The program's mission was to provide advocacy to survivors of interpersonal violence, including stalking, relationship violence, and sexual assault. (Although the program kept its original name, "Victim Advocate Program," as the profession evolved, advocates referred to "victims" as "survivors" to underscore their strengths.) The advocates, who were available twenty-four hours a day, served FSU students or anyone victimized on campus. The Victim Advocate Program offered a broad range of support services, such as accompanying a survivor to the hospital, doctor's office, police department, judicial proceedings, or counselor's office; contacting the student's instructors to arrange for academic accommodations; referring a student to individual counseling or support groups; arranging for alternative housing for the student or lodging for parents who come to offer support; and maintaining contact with the police, state attorney's office, and the FSU Office of Student's Rights and Responsibilities.

Staff at the Victim Advocate Program consisted of the director (who also was an assistant dean of students), the assistant director, five on-call advocates, and a select group of volunteers who facilitated educational presentations, staffed information booths at public events, offered office assistance, and conducted special projects. All staff and volunteers embraced the universal credo that advocates should use a survivor-centered approach at all times. Of critical importance was the guiding principle that survivors must be believed because skepticism might compound the trauma of assault.

LINDSEY RICKARD, ASSISTANT DIRECTOR OF THE VICTIM ADVOCATE PROGRAM

When Lindsey Rickard graduated from FSU with a bachelor of arts degree in art history, she had one goal in mind: find a job with health insurance immediately! A confident "go-getter," Lindsey quickly found a position with great benefits at a marketing and public-relations firm specializing in nonprofits. A spunky twenty-one-year-old with flawless peach-toned skin, a sporty bobbed haircut, and a crisp professional wardrobe, she was a gifted fund-raiser. She successfully ran campaigns for nonprofits and taught volunteers and staff at nonprofit organizations to run their own campaigns. Thanks to Lindsey, the money flowed. But she wanted more. Working for the sake of money was not enough. She found herself captivated by the agencies she served, in particular those providing services to sexual trauma survivors.

In her free time, Lindsey volunteered to provide direct services to survivors, and in exchange she received extensive survivor advocacy training through a hospital-based sexual trauma unit. "This work lights a fire under me like I have never had before," Lindsey declared to her fund-raising friends. To no one's surprise, Lindsey transitioned from fund-raising to a speaker's bureau position where she educated middle and high school students about sexual health and violence prevention.

After about three years of immersion in that program, Lindsey set her sights on an open position as assistant director of the FSU Victim Advocate Program. She landed the job, and nearly one year into the work she still loved survivor advocacy even more than the day she started. Lindsey was an unshakable and fierce advocate for survivors. She knew that one out of every four college women has been raped or experienced an attempted rape and that the United States has the world's highest rape rate of the countries that publish such statistics.

Survivors needed to have control over decision making because of the trauma and because so much control had been taken from them, so Lindsey gave survivors space but also made herself available for every step in the process, night or day. And in Lindsey's mind, a survivor could not hear the words "I believe you and I am here for you" too often. She defended her clients if an insensitive police investigator became too aggressive. She prearranged for a survivor to signal subtly if she wanted a break, and when Lindsey saw a pinky finger raise in the air or the survivor touch her ear, she immediately asked for a break. Lindsey developed a professional but powerful bond with her clients; it was clear to anyone watching. She loved the work so much that she planned to pursue a master's in social work beginning in the summer to further advance her skills.

JAN TAYLOR, INVESTIGATOR FOR THE VICTIM ADVOCATE PROGRAM

Jan Taylor, who had just celebrated her fortieth birthday, was a petite but powerful woman with short blond hair and soft blue eyes. When the Victim Advocate Program budgeted for a full-time sexual assault investigator, Jan was the obvious choice. She had graduated from the police academy and had pursued training in special investigations before joining the campus police force. She conducted herself professionally and compassionately with sexual assault survivors, making her a respected member of the campus police and the Victim Advocate Program. Jan did not wear a uniform when she worked. She wanted survivors to feel comfortable in her presence and preferred neatly pressed slacks and a button-down shirt.

It was a Sunday afternoon in early February, and Lindsey and Jan braced themselves against a chilly winter breeze as they walked together from their parked cars into the residence hall. They were responding to a crisis call involving sexual trauma. The survivor's name was Rachel Conway.

Rachel's concerned resident adviser, Abby Greenfield, greeted them nervously in the lobby and led them to Rachel's dorm room. Rachel made eye contact with Lindsey and Jan as she opened the door. Everything about Rachel Conway was understated. She had pulled her short dark hair tightly into a ponytail that looked almost like a bun. Her unadorned skin was apple-flesh colored, and she wore well-loved blue jeans, white tennis shoes, and a plain knit top. Her room was organized and tidy, with a couple of family pictures carefully placed on her desk and bedside table. After closing the door behind Jan and Lindsey, Rachel walked to her bed and sat stoically as Jan and Lindsey found chairs. Jan grabbed a desk chair and moved far enough away from Rachel that she sat below Rachel's eye level and slightly off center.

Jan is so considerate, Lindsey thought, *she never towers over our clients or intimidates them when she takes a report.*

Lindsey pulled a second chair over to the bed and placed it across from Rachel.

Jan allowed Rachel to tell her story in her own time. Rachel was heading back to the dorm from the student social center when a man jumped her from behind and pushed her down a stairwell. When she looked up, she saw a man with a black ski mask, black jeans, a black T-shirt, and black shoes hovering over her. The man held a three-inch knife with a black handle to her throat and began to touch her breasts and pull down her pants. Suddenly there was a noise, and when the man turned his head in the direction of the sound, Rachel kneed him in the crotch, poked him in the eyes, and fled to the dorm.

At that point, Rachel, who had told her story stone-faced, suddenly crumbled into quiet sobs. Lindsey sensed that Rachel did not want to be touched, but she quietly said, "I am so sorry that this happened to you."

After a few moments, Rachel regained her composure.

"So what happened after you ran?" Jan asked.

"Came here," Rachel said.

"Who was here?"

"No one."

"So then what did you do?"

"I called the campus police," Rachel said.

"You mean today?" Jan asked.

"No, yesterday," Rachel said, looking out of the window, "but the officer just came and laughed. He just laughed."

What! Lindsey thought. *We have worked so hard to educate officers about client treatment. They are always so great. How can there still be officers who just don't get it?*

"I am so sorry," Lindsey said.

Jan looked up from her notepad. Her brow furrowed, and Lindsey knew she was deep in thought. "Can you remember the officer's name?" Jan asked.

"No," Rachel said.

"Can you remember if he was white or black?"

"No."

"Do you remember anything at all that could help me find him?"

"No. No, I just don't remember," Rachel said.

"It's alright if you don't remember; this is a lot to recall," Lindsey said. "Do you need a break?"

"No," Rachel said quietly, "I'm okay."

"Well, then if it's okay," Jan said, "I have a few more questions."

Rachel nodded her head in agreement.

Jan then asked a series of follow-up question before she flipped through the pages of her notebook and said, "I think I have enough for now. I'll give you time to rest."

Lindsey could tell Jan was troubled. She had asked too many follow-up questions. She would normally just take the statement, ask a couple of questions, and then end it, but this time her approach was different. She seemed to be checking inconsistencies in Rachel's story.

If Rachel noticed what Jan was doing, Lindsey couldn't tell. Rachel seemed to answer what questions she could and simply to decline when she could not remember.

As the interview ended, the three women agreed to meet again on Monday in Lindsey's office. Jan almost always met clients at Lindsey's office for follow-up interviews because it was more private and cozy than the police station. Lindsey had plenty of artwork on the wall for clients to stare at to take their minds away from the horror they experienced. She also had a large basket full of small toys and stress-reduction gadgets for nervous hands. After handing Rachel her business card, Jan gently excused herself.

Lindsey stayed a few minutes longer to explain to Rachel the law enforcement process, review the services available from the university, and provide anything that Rachel needed that moment.

"I don't expect you to remember all of this," Lindsey said softly to Rachel, "so I will give you an information booklet that reiterates everything we talk about. I am marking specific pages for you that I think will be helpful."

Lindsey marked in the booklet, looked at Rachel, and continued, "Please know that whatever you decide to do with your case, I will support you in your decision. You are the expert on your life; I will back you up. Our services are available to you until you graduate or until you tell me to go away! I work for you."

When Lindsey added "until you tell me to go away," Rachel nodded and smiled briefly. Lindsey hoped she was starting to establish rapport with her new client. Some of Jan's questions seemed to challenge her client, but Lindsey had learned long ago to remove her views from the situation and meet clients "where they are." It was easy for people to second guess and say, "Oh, that's not what I would do." *You never know how you react until it happens to you*, Lindsey thought. *There's no such thing as good judgment or bad judgment. It happened. The client and I go from there.*

Lindsey asked a couple of questions about Rachel's support system to make sure she would be okay. Although Rachel's family had lived in Tallahassee for years, the family had moved out of state in Rachel's junior year. Rachel's mother had died the summer before she came to college, but Rachel stayed in close contact with her father. He knew about the assault and was supportive.

Rachel explained that her boyfriend lived only thirty miles away in Thomasville, Georgia, but because neither she nor her boyfriend had a car, they might as well have been three hundred miles apart. He was concerned about Rachel and promised to rent a car and visit the following weekend. Rachel shared a dorm suite with three other girls who knew little more than her name.

Lindsey left Rachel in the care of her resident adviser and was heading back to her car when her cell phone rang. It was Jan. "Hey, Lindsey, can you come over to the stairwell where Rachel said she was attacked. I want you to see something."

That's odd, Lindsey thought and then said, "Sure, no problem. I'll be right there."

It was about 6:30 in the evening when Lindsey arrived at the top of the stairwell and spotted Jan surveying the area below. Students walked by the area periodically.

This area is a lot more visible than I thought, Lindsey reflected.

"This is where she said it happened, right?" Jan asked.

"Yes," Lindsey said, "This is where it happened."

"I remembered it being a little more closed in than it actually is," Jan said, mostly to herself. She pulled out her cell phone, looked at the screen, and then clipped it back on her belt. "It's about 6:40, about the right time. Still some daylight left," she said, looking at the sky.

They both quietly observed as laughing students walked by.

"It's pretty rare for someone to remember so much detail," Jan said aloud. "She even remembered the color of the handle of the knife . . . "

Lindsey looked at her but didn't say anything. *I believe her*, she thought. *I know it's odd, but I believe her. Women don't just lie about rape. The price they pay for coming forward is too great.*

"But I guess it's possible," Jan said, measuring the area with a tape measure she pulled from her belt and writing the figures in a small notebook. "But I gotta level with you, Lindsey. It's a little strange to think that someone was attacked in this fairly open space, with people milling around and a little daylight still in the sky."

"I believe her," Lindsey said firmly. *No wonder only 4 percent of college women report sexual assault to police*, she thought. *And I know Jan is on our team!*

"Look," Jan said, stepping closer to Lindsey, "I am not saying she's lying. I am just saying that the circumstances—"

"I don't think anything is beyond belief," Lindsey interrupted with conviction. "I have heard of situations beyond bizarre that were proven to be true."

"Yeah, me too," Jan said nodding her head once in affirmation.

"I believe her, "Lindsey repeated. "It is possible, although maybe not plausible, but . . . "

"Possible," Jan said, adding her voice to Lindsey's. She closed her notebook and moved toward the steps. "I'll keep looking for what's possible then."

"Thanks," Lindsey said, smiling.

FOLLOW-UP

The next morning Lindsey discovered that Jan had left a phone message for her at six that morning. "I found something in the Conway case. Can you swing by the station sometime this morning?"

Does she ever sleep? Lindsey mused as she looked at her calendar.

Lindsey was supposed to be the guest lecturer at a freshman class that morning, but she found an MSW student volunteer to cover for her and walked over to campus security.

Jan looked exhausted, and the mood was somber as she led Lindsey into a tiny room with audio-video equipment. "I want to show you something," she said, and then she played a handful of video clips that showed Rachel at various locations as she walked on campus that Saturday evening.

She found it, Lindsey thought. *She got him on tape.* Lindsey held her breath as the video recording captured Rachel approaching the stairwell where she was attacked.

Lindsey was on edge waiting for the perpetrator to knock Rachel down the steps. But nothing happened. Rachel walked right by the stairwell she had identified as the location of the assault.

Lindsey started to speak, but Jan said, "Wait a minute," as she fiddled with the video equipment. "I pulled the footage and watched one hour before the incident and one hour after the incident, but there's nothing on film. You can see for yourself. The timeline matches. She walked exactly where she told us at the exact times she told us, but there's no attack on the stairwell."

They watched as the video, on fast-forward mode, sped through time. Lindsey felt a burning in her chest. "So what are you saying?"

Jan moved away from the video machine and sat beside Lindsey. "Look, I am not trying to be a jerk."

"I understand, Jan, but you are trying to tell me something," Lindsey said more sharply than she intended. "You saw her. She was physically crying. It wasn't just Hollywood tears. Something happened. Maybe she changed the story to be more socially acceptable—"

Jan nodded her head. "I believe something happened, but not the incident she reported."

After a moment's hesitation, Jan said, "There's more. I checked and double-checked and triple-checked the telephone records for Saturday and Sunday. There were no calls to the campus police during that time frame reporting a sexual assault. I just don't think she made the call on Saturday."

Lindsey was bewildered. *The FBI found that people are more likely to fake their own death than to file a false sexual assault report! So what are we missing? How can this make sense?*

"Let's talk to her again," Lindsey said.

"Oh, you better believe I have to," Jan said with authority. "Listen, Lindsey, this case has gone all the way up the line of command. You know, we throw everything we've got into a stranger attack on campus. And once Rachel said an officer came and laughed, well, it's gone to the top. I have to talk to her, and I have to get some answers."

"Jan," Lindsey pleaded, "you know that the worst thing that can happen to a survivor is to be challenged. Maybe she did modify the story to make it more socially acceptable, but now she'll be hesitant to come forward with the truth if you press her too hard."

"Lindsey, we need answers."

You need answers, Lindsey thought. *I don't, because I believe her. At least, I think so. I am supposed to believe her, right? I am her advocate. Survivors must be believed.*

"I'm not sure if you should be in the room when I question Rachel," Jan said to Lindsey. "Normally, I know you stay by your client's side for everything, but I don't want Rachel to lump you in with the police department at this point. As her advocate, you do not want to be associated with the police department's doubt."

"I think that's a great idea," Lindsey said, "and I will be right outside the door if she calls for me."

"Whatever you think is best," Jan said as she began to gather her things.

Lindsey felt conflicted about whether she should accompany Rachel during Jan's questioning, but she was late for a meeting and decided the answer might become more apparent with time.

Later that afternoon Lindsey looked at her watch and gasped. *Where has the day gone?* she wondered, as she jumped up from her office desk chair and then hesitated at the threshold of her door. *This discussion isn't going to be easy. I want to support Rachel and be by her side, but I don't want her to see me grouped with the police department.*

ON THE OTHER SIDE OF THE DOOR

At the beginning of the meeting, Lindsey started the conversation by asking Rachel about her well-being. Was she eating? Was she sleeping? Was she able to get to class? The questions reduced Rachel to tears, and Lindsey again was struck by the wholeheartedness of her pain. She seemed so childlike.

"I want you to know that you are safe here," she whispered, trying to sooth Rachel with her voice. Lindsey sensed that Rachel still was not comfortable with Lindsey sitting too close to her. Rachel had an invisible shield that said, "That's far enough!" and Lindsey wanted to honor that warning.

Rachel cried for a few seconds and then stopped. "I can't sleep," she sniffed. "And the nightmares have gotten even worse than they were before."

"Before?" Lindsey repeated, trying to understand. "When did the nightmares start, Rachel?"

It's been mon—ths," Rachel moaned, convulsing.

Months? Lindsey questioned. *What happened to her months ago? I wonder if she's reliving a past sexual trauma . . .*

Rachel pulled a tissue from the box that Lindsey placed in front of her and mopped her tears. She had regained her composure.

Jan nodded imperceptibly. Lindsey left the room but hovered right outside of the door as she promised. *I feel that I should be in there for her,* she thought, *but I don't want her to think that I don't believe her!*

Seconds later Jan came out of the conference room. Lindsey knew something had gone wrong. Jan was flushed. "She wants to talk to you," Jan said. "This time she said the guy who attacked her was in his twenties or thirties. How would she know that if he was wearing a ski mask? I told her straight up that I believed that something happened, but I needed to know everything, and that's when she asked to talk to you."

As soon as Lindsey opened the door to the conference room, Rachel met her eyes. She looked like a frightened child, and Lindsey saw big tears well up. Rachel's shoulders quaked as she wept into her hands. Jan sat at the far end of the table. Lindsey went over and sat by Rachel. "What are you upset about right now?"

"They don't believe me," Rachel wailed. "I just want to move on with my life. I just want to move on . . . "

"I believe you," Lindsey said steadily and then more firmly, "I don't doubt that something has happened to you." *I wonder if she hears me hedging. I do believe something happened. Less than 2 percent of all sexual assault reports are false, so I definitely believe something happened. But what happened, and why won't she just tell me?*

After a minute, Rachel recovered and looked resolute again.

Lindsey took her cue, "Rachel, has anything like this ever happened to you before?"

Rachel stared glassy-eyed at a pink, squishy stress ball that she was kneading vigorously. After a long pause, she looked directly at Lindsey and said, "No."

Rachel then fidgeted in her chair. Lindsey could tell she was uncomfortable. *Why am I struggling to connect with this client?* Lindsey wondered. *It's normally so much easier for me.*

Lindsey felt at a loss about how to help Rachel process her experience and become a healthy and successful student again. *How DO you find resolution in a case that's damaging to both the student and the community?* Lindsey wondered.

She felt herself starting to panic because she could hear Rachel starting to lose heart, and she knew Jan was exasperated and getting a lot of pressure from her superiors.

The myth of excessive false reports of sexual violence is rampant, she thought. *The last thing this program needs is for the Conway case to become the exception that makes the rule, proving that people commonly lie about sexual assaults. How am I supposed to believe her? I want to believe her. But should I?*

5

I KNEW THIS INTERNSHIP THING
WOULD BLOW UP!

Gecole Harley and Terry A. Wolfer

"Are we still going to let him stay even after he did all that to Rene?" Supervisor Lamina Koroma was standing in Jennifer Meadow's doorway.

Jennifer knew immediately that she was referring to Scott Campbell, a student intern in their refugee resettlement program. She tried to sound firm, although the pitch of her voice was a little higher than normal. "I have a heart to really see Scott through this. We have only a couple of weeks to go. I would hate to see him drop out of the social work program because of this."

Development of this decision case was supported in part by funding from the University of South Carolina College of Social Work. It was prepared solely to provide material for class discussion and not to suggest either effective or ineffective handling of the situation depicted. Although the case is based on field research regarding an actual situation, names and certain facts may have been disguised to protect confidentiality. The authors thank the anonymous case reporter for cooperation in making this account available for the benefit of social work students and instructors.

Lamina looked as if she had just gotten a whiff of something that smelled bad. "See," she said accusingly, "I KNEW this internship thing would blow up!"

IMMIGRATION AND REFUGEE MINISTRIES ASSOCIATION

The Immigration and Refugee Ministries Association (IRMA) had been in operation for nearly twenty years. It began when several Atlanta-area churches banded together to help resettle Montagnard and later Somali Bantu refugees. The churches were motivated by scriptural teachings about caring for aliens and strangers (Leviticus 19:33–34; Matthew 25:35), and IRMA provided a means to organize and administer their efforts. IRMA eventually established several satellite offices across the state. The president's office was in Atlanta, and the vice president's office was in Macon. Other satellite offices with area managers and staff included Stone Mountain and Clarkston.

The organizational structure at each local site had three layers. For example, the Stone Mountain office included four case managers, two translators, and one area manager who oversaw local operations. The area manager reported to both the vice president in Macon and the president in Atlanta.

Beginning in late 2004, the Stone Mountain office experienced a constant churning of staff after the longtime area manager retired. One of the two case managers reluctantly served as interim area manager for three months. After disappointing candidate searches, one infamous bad hire that lasted less than six months, and much cajoling, the interim area manager was eventually hired as the permanent area manager.

KEY IRMA STAFF

While a young adult, Lamina Koroma had come to the United States from Sierra Leone as a refugee. She subsequently had earned a master's degree in women's studies. Now in her early forties, Lamina had served as the interim area manager for the Stone Mountain office twice before she finally relented and accepted the position permanently. She had hesitated to accept the position because she felt burdened with immediate and extended family responsibilities. She was the married mother of two children but also looked out for other family members who had not fared so well in the United States.

Jennifer Meadows was a petite, young-looking twenty-five-year-old whose bright voice and easy laugh quickly filled the room with her vibrant energy. Just two years earlier, she had earned her MSW from the University of Texas at Austin. After completing the MSW program, she had moved with her husband to Georgia and accepted a position as case manager for refugee resettlement at IRMA. As case manager, Jennifer performed a variety of tasks. For example, she prepared for incoming refugees by securing donations, ensuring houses were fully supplied as required by federal regulations, and coordinating volunteers from congregations to assist them. Following their arrival, she helped clients access transportation services, health screenings, and English-language classes.

Scott Campbell, a second-career, thirty-three-year-old MSW student, had just completed his first year of studies at the University of Georgia in Athens. As the son of professional nongovernmental organization workers, Scott had been a high school teacher. After teaching for eight years, he decided that social work seemed a better fit for his personality and values. He was a tall, thin, lanky fellow who took pride in a minimalist, international traveler persona. He often dressed the part—with baggy khaki cargo shorts and T-shirts that reflected a flippant attitude toward the agency dress code.

Rene Cassidy, also in her thirties, had earned a bachelor's degree in psychology and immediately launched a career in social work that had been satisfying for the past seven years. She had been at IRMA for only one year, and IRMA had provided her first experience in the field of immigration and refugee resettlement. She was in charge of implementing a summer program for the children of Somali Bantu refugees.

RESETTLEMENT POPULATIONS

During its two-decade existence, IRMA had served a variety of refugee populations, including Somali Bantu from Somali in East Africa and Montagnard from Vietnam. Although they differed in significant ways, both groups had long histories of minority status, discrimination, and marginalization within their countries of origin. Like many refugee populations resettled in the United States, both had experienced the trauma of war and violent conflict, forced relocation, and the difficult living conditions of refugee camps. The Somali Bantu, with their history of enslavement and persecution, were especially vulnerable when civil war broke out in Somalia in the 1990s. The Montagnards, as indigenous peoples of the Central Highlands of Vietnam, were culturally distinct from mainstream Vietnamese and other highlanders such as the Hmong. Because they had collaborated with the Americans during the Vietnam War, the Montagnards were additionally targeted as traitors and US spies by the Communist government after the war. Although many Montagnard refugees were Christian, most Somali Bantu were Muslim.

GREAT EXPECTATIONS

Jennifer was meandering back to her office after an intense meeting when she saw Rene at the far end of the hall race-walking toward her. At Rene's heels was a slender young man Jennifer recognized as an English as a Second Language volunteer, although she didn't know his name. Their obvious excitement was infectious, and Jennifer felt her face brighten.

Rene skidded to a halt inches from Jennifer's face.

"Hey!" she said breathlessly.

"Hey," Jennifer replied, smiling and waiting.

"I have an awesome proposal for you," Rene announced.

"Oh, really?" Jennifer replied, sounding playfully suspicious.

"Yep! Remember when the agency was toying with the idea of getting an MSW intern this fall?" Rene asked, looking conspiratorially at the young man at her side. "Well, this is Scott, and he is the One—although he has to come this summer instead of the fall!"

"Well, the agency has certainly considered taking on an MSW intern," Jennifer said. "So let me talk to Lamina and see what she says." Although Jennifer had only recently graduated from an MSW program herself, she was willing to accept a new challenge.

Rene and Scott immediately began to celebrate, with fist pumps and broad smiles.

"Of course," Jennifer hedged, "if Lamina agrees. . . . I mean, I can't give you permission myself."

"Oh NO-ooo," Rene said with an exaggerated drawl. Jennifer could tell that Rene and Scott already assumed it was a done deal.

It wasn't. When Jennifer initially presented the idea to Lamina, Lamina was not enthusiastic. Jennifer knew that Lamina was trying to dig out of the work that accumulated while leadership was in transition. Adding the MSW internship was not a small project. The university required that the student intern work at the facility five days a week, eight hours a day, during an intensive twelve-week summer block beginning in May. It was already February. For a moment, Jennifer thought Lamina was going to reject the idea, but instead she said, "I don't think it's a good idea, but it's your decision. You're the MSW. You handle it."

"Of course!" Jennifer said, taking pride in her professional competence.

ARRANGING THE PLACEMENT

The demands of Jennifer's immigration work never stopped, and there were so many people pleading for help. But amid the usual chaos and pressure, she took steps to prepare for the possible placement. She went to Lamina for advice a few times, but Lamina usually said, "You're the MSW, you handle it." *Poor Lamina works almost around the clock,* Jennifer observed, *and she's still buried. I can figure out this contract on my own and take at least one burden off of her shoulders. Now I remember why I turned down that administrative job at Catholic Social Services. And thank goodness I had the sense to turn down the area manager's job here at IRMA.*

About a month after their first discussion, Jennifer arranged a meeting with Scott and Rene. Scott brought paperwork from the university's Field Office, and they all read it together and filled it out as best they could. They agreed that Rene would serve as the preceptor for Scott's daily tasks, and each signed off on the plan. Then Jennifer took the paperwork to Lamina to get her signature and to ask what to do next. Lamina signed off and instructed Jennifer to supply a copy to Human Resources. Finally, Jennifer faxed the paperwork to the Field Office.

THE INTERVIEW

The second week of April arrived too quickly for Jennifer. With only two weeks before the start of the summer internship session, Jennifer forced herself to find time for an interview with Scott.

On the day of the interview, Jennifer heard Scott coming before she saw him. He was wearing muted orange flip flops that smacked as he strode down the hall toward her office. His Khaki cargo shorts were holey, and his tan cotton shirt hung unevenly around his waist because it had not been ironed. He carried a battered leather briefcase with patches of leather literally tearing away from the steel frame. He plopped the briefcase on top of Jennifer's desk with a thud and then casually fell into one of two chairs that faced her desk.

"Hey!" Jennifer greeted Scott, musing silently about the peculiar juxtaposition of his casual attire with the once stately briefcase.

"Good afternoon," Scott responded gruffly.

"Scott," Jennifer began, "I just need to make sure that you understand that the contract with the university has not been completed and approved. We're still ironing out details. I just want you to understand that this is not a done deal even though we have talked about allowing you to start in May."

"Ehhh," Scott said, waving his hand dismissively, "it's not the first time the Bureaucracy has tried to screw me out of stuff. I can handle myself. You know that the school originally promised me that I could do my internship at the agency where I worked?"

"No," Jennifer said, "I didn't know."

"Well, they did," Scott said sharply, "but then once I moved here, they refused. I tried to tell them how strapped I am for cash—just returned from an overseas project where I got only a small stipend to barely pay my expenses. But the system screwed me. I couldn't take my internship in the fall and spring with my classmates because I had to work to pay tuition and living expenses. Now," he snorted, "I'm cramming in this block semester and trying to live off of my savings."

"I am so sorry," Jennifer said. Her heart went out to him. She could imagine what it was like to be a starving student.

"Eh, I'll get through it," he said and then added, "so Rene said I could go ahead and start next week. I think this placement will work under the circumstances."

That's rather presumptuous, Jennifer thought. *He said that as if it were a done deal.* But she didn't say anything. *He's really going through a tough time,* Jennifer allowed. They proceeded to talk about what he would do, what her role would be, and how he needed to keep track of his hours and have Rene sign off on them as his preceptor.

PROPER CHANNELS

With the contract resolved, Scott began his block placement the first week of May as he and Rene had planned. Jennifer fortunately didn't have to worry about keeping Scott occupied. He and Rene were frantically trying to launch the Somali Bantu children's summer program. Jennifer saw Scott only once that first week as he was running through the hall. He stopped for a minute to say hi.

The following Monday afternoon, Jennifer was working at her desk, half-listening for Scott to check in for their supervision session, when there was a knock at the open door. Jennifer assumed she would look up and see Scott, but she was wrong. Instead, Lamina's assistant said, "Lamina wants to see you in her office."

Jennifer had barely stepped into Lamina's office when Lamina asked, "I thought you told me everything was in order with the contract?" She sounded both fearful and agitated.

"What?" Taken aback, Jennifer didn't even know which contract Lamina was talking about. Jennifer walked toward her desk and sat down in one of the two guest chairs.

"You went above me to try to get this passed," Lamina said.

Jennifer immediately wanted to retreat. *Lamina and I have always had such a good working relationship as colleagues,* Jennifer thought, *and not much has changed since she became my supervisor.*

As Lamina rapidly listed the particulars, Jennifer realized that she had not "gone through proper channels" because she didn't even know there were proper channels to go through to contract for an MSW intern, and Lamina had not indicated that there were any to follow. The vice president's office in Macon was apparently supposed to be actively involved in the process of contracting and was unhappy when the contract was presented to him as if it were a done deal. He needed to sign all contracts. Jennifer felt rumblings in the pit of her stomach. She took a deep breath and leaned toward Lamina as she spoke.

"Listen, Lamina, I was trying to help. I thought you delegated that to me . . . " Jennifer's voice drifted off as Lamina started to shake her head no.

"I never delegated that to you," Lamina responded curtly.

"Well, I thought you said for me to handle it, and I wanted to follow through so you wouldn't be bothered. I am so very sorry."

"Jennifer," Lamina looked annoyed, "I really took a tongue lashing over this thing, and I didn't need more on my plate. You know how things are around here for me. I was the interim director twice, although I didn't want the job. As I tried to get my feet on the ground, the agency kept cutting the budget. Staff members were furious with the constant influx of leadership, with the budget cuts, with the growing amount of work. They started leaving in droves." Lamina quickly took in breath and continued, "On top of everything else, every waking moment there's a case audit around the corner, and I just got this job, officially. And then the church volunteers think that they have all of the answers. And you know things are chaotic at home with my in-laws, my kids . . . and now my mother's sick." Lamina stopped suddenly and looked out of the window, as if to collect herself. "I didn't need to have one more thing explode in my face. I didn't need to be called out by my supervisor for having staff do something as critical as contract negotiation."

Jennifer felt her insides shriveling. She spoke slowly. "I do not want this contract to ruin our relationship. I'm not even going to do this if it's going to be that bad between us. I will tell Scott and Rene that it just isn't going to work out. He only started last week. We can just cut our losses now if you think that's best."

After an uncomfortable conversation that lasted for about half an hour, Jennifer said, "Forget it, let's not do this if it's going to drive a wedge between us. Lamina, it means more to me that we have a good working relationship."

"Do whatever you think," Lamina seemed to soften, perhaps out of exhaustion. "You have the MSW."

After some discussion, they agreed to resend the contract through the proper channels and wait to see if it was approved.

Back at her office, Jennifer took time to settle her nerves. Although she tried hard to respect superiors and follow protocol, she felt angry and even betrayed by Lamina. *She said it was OK earlier. I was just trying to help out. Now she's blaming me.* Finally, she decided to persevere. She couldn't disappoint Scott. He really needed this internship to work out.

FIELD VISIT

One week later Sandra Pickens, the university field liaison assigned to work with Jennifer and Scott, was scheduled to visit the agency. Rene unfortunately could not attend the meeting because she needed to be on-site at the summer program, but Jennifer was technically the supervisor anyway. Before the meeting, Jennifer spent a couple of frustrating hours rewriting the learning contract that Scott had developed. The sentences within the body of the contract were fragments, and Scott had not listed learning tasks for each of the university's objectives. It was not professional work, in Jennifer's opinion, and though she knew it wasn't her job to rewrite it, she wanted to spruce it up before the field liaison came.

As Jennifer, Scott, and Sandra sat around a small round table, Sandra began pleasantly, "Scott, I am so glad to finally meet you. I've heard a little about the agency from Jennifer, but please tell me what you're doing here. Tell me what you are learning."

Scott had been reclined in his chair, picking at the cuticles of his nails, but he suddenly sat up and said gruffly, "I'm not learning anything." Then he talked about how he already had a master's in education, how the university had cheated him out of the opportunity to get internship credit at his place of employment, and how he was strapped financially because he was required to pay for the internship as a class.

"It's pretty hard for me to worry about finding air conditioning for the refugees here when my own air conditioning broke last week, and I don't even have gas money to get to work."

Jennifer took the outburst in stride because she and the rest of the staff had heard Scott's troubles before, but it took Sandra a moment to collect herself.

"Well, it sounds as if you have experienced some disappointments and frustrations getting to this placement, and I have no control over that piece, but let's see if we can make this experience a good one for you. Tell me about your classes so that we can make sure to incorporate class learning into field learning."

"I don't learn anything in class," Scott grumbled. "Sometimes I think I ought to just quit the MSW program, just cut my losses."

Remembering some of her own frustrations with courses that did not challenge, Jennifer asked, "What can we give you to read to help?"

"I don't need to read anything else," Scott sounded haughty. "I've read everything."

Jennifer felt her face flush. *Oh,* she thought, *I think I overstepped my boundaries. I meant to be helpful.*

"Have you read Perlman?" Sandra asked Scott.

But why do I feel as if I overstepped my boundaries? I am his supervisor, Jennifer thought to herself.

"Yes," Scott said irritated, "I've read a lot of his work."

Now he's ticked off and will be difficult to work with. I'll apologize tomorrow, Jennifer thought, comforting herself.

"Her," Sandra corrected, "HER work."

"Oh, oh," Scott said. He opened his briefcase, which was sitting on the table, and random pieces of paper spilled out. The clutter was unsystematic and disturbing to Jennifer. *How does he know how to retrieve all of that information?* she wondered.

Jennifer thought she saw concern in Sandra's face, too.

Scott scribbled Perlman's name on a scrap of paper that already had other scribbling on it and said, "I'll look it up sometime."

Sandra then turned back to the learning contract, which they hashed out, although the process felt more like wrestling than collaboration.

WHO'S THE BOSS?

Nearly a month into the internship, Jennifer hardly saw Scott. He was supposed to spend two days each week with Jennifer, but he never came to Jennifer's office to request assignments. When Jennifer saw him around the office, he seemed too busy to talk to her. *I don't want to be a micromanager,* Jennifer thought. *He's a responsible adult. He knows what he should be doing.*

On the rare occasion that Scott would drop by, it was usually to complain about Rene's management of the program. "She's only worried about forms, forms, forms, and she does nothing to recruit volunteers. Does all that paper serve anyone other than the System?" Scott asked. It was clear he thought it was a rhetorical question.

"Well," Jennifer said, "without documentation we can't get grants, and without grants we can't get money, so the forms do serve a purpose, although I agree they can be onerous."

I am still struggling to complete the internship contract for you, Jennifer thought. *Surely you must think that form's important!*

"It's dangerous over there," Scott said. Jennifer knew he was referring to the children's program site. "We don't have enough supervisors for the children, and someone is going to get hurt." Scott slapped his hand on his knee for emphasis. "Rene needs to get us volunteers and not worry so much about the paperwork. That's what I would do if I were the program director."

TROUBLED TIMES

In the third week of June, Jennifer saw Rene making copies at the copy machine, and she approached her to chat. Jennifer had seen Scott earlier that day and had asked, "How's Rene?" In response, Scott had rolled his eyes, said, "Who knows?" and kept walking.

Jennifer knew the pressure of starting a new program could be overwhelming, and she wanted to check in with Rene, but before she opened her mouth, Rene said, "He is really aggravating me today."

"You want me to arrange for a peace talk?" Jennifer asked.

"No. It's fine," Rene said as she grabbed her copies. "See ya, Jennifer."

But by the next week things deteriorated further between Rene and Scott. Although they had begun the summer block as friends, it seemed they now quarreled almost incessantly. At least every couple of days, Scott or Rene would visit Jennifer separately to complain about the other.

"We don't have enough volunteers," Scott groused on one such occasion, "because she's not recruiting them. She's too busy filling out paperwork," using a mocking tone when he said "paperwork." "I'm busy taking out the trash because she hasn't recruited any volunteers. Meanwhile, there is one less person watching the children while I'm out."

Later that same day Rene stomped into Jennifer's office to register her own complaints. "I'm trying to make sure that we don't get nailed to the cross during an audit, and all I get from Scott is, 'Why do we even write it down? Who cares?'"

Jennifer gave Rene a moment to calm herself and then asked, "Would you like for me to try and help build a bridge?"

"No," Rene replied, "we can work it out."

Nevertheless, the cycle of complaints continued and even escalated. Scott began writing disparaging comments about Rene in the volunteer comment book that staff used to monitor volunteer relations. The scribbled notes were unmistakably in Scott's handwriting, and a few times he even signed his name. For her part, Rene began to rant to other staff members about her frustrations with Scott, which made everyone uncomfortable. Jennifer allowed both Scott and Rene to vent in her office, but finally, after another week of bad days, Jennifer asked Rene softly, "I have plenty of work for him to do here. He can work here with me five days a week, and then you two won't have to work together with the children's program."

"No way," Rene stiffened. "I paid for him; I need to use him," she said, referring to the church contribution used to pay Scott a small stipend. "And besides, I don't have enough people to help supervise the children as it is."

Should I just use my prerogative as field instructor and step in? Jennifer wondered. *No,* she decided, *you need to honor their desire to work things out in their own way.*

Jennifer returned to her desk to find a telephone message from the university inquiring about the status of the contract. *God give me strength*, Jennifer thought as she picked up the stack of forms on her desk that represented drafts of the contract.

"IT'S OVER!"

Jennifer had just sat down to plow through weeks of paperwork that had accumulated on her desk when Rene barged in, stopping just inside the doorway, and bellowed, "It's OVER!" She looked feverish with rage. "I'm wanting to call it quits, Jennifer. I want him out. He even threatened to call CPS on me . . . on the program. CPS! I mean it. I want him out!!!"

Jennifer didn't even try to argue. It was the second week in July, and she sensed it coming. "I understand, Rene, I do. But I am wondering if it would be okay with you if he stays to finish up with me. I mean, at this point he has only a couple of weeks remaining, and he's already thinking about quitting the MSW program. But if you want him out of the agency, I will respect your decision."

"If you can put up with him, then . . . ," and without finishing she backhanded the air in front of her with disgust and backed out the door.

About an hour later, Scott walked into Jennifer's office, dropped his briefcase on Jennifer's desk, and said gruffly, "This is not working out."

Jennifer was surprised by his tone. She expected him to be a little more worried. "Well, Scott," she said, "there's a lot you haven't done with case management, so you can just spend the final weeks here with me, if you want."

Scott muttered gruffly, "Let's just get it over with. All I have been doing since I started the MSW program is jump through hoops anyway."

After Scott left the room, Jennifer sat staring out the window, thinking about the situation. *Gee*, she thought, *I sort of expected a sigh of relief and at least one expression of gratitude. But I have a heart to really see him through this. I don't want him to leave the MSW program because of this internship.* She had heard from other people in the agency, more impartial people, that the conflict was a personality clash. Neither was totally at fault, and both were partially to blame.

"Are we still going to let him stay even after he did all that to Rene?" Lamina was standing in Jennifer's doorway. Her question was not really a question; Jennifer could tell. *How in the world did she even find out?* Jennifer wondered. She hadn't even thought about talking to Lamina about the situation. She was trying to avoid bothering Lamina with anything related to the MSW internship. Jennifer felt frustrated. *I was getting things sorted out so that Lamina wouldn't have to be bothered again.* Jennifer tried to sound firm, although the pitch of her voice was a little higher than normal. "I have a heart to really see Scott through this. We have only a couple of weeks to go. I would hate to see him drop out of the social work program because of this."

Lamina looked as if she had just gotten a whiff of something that smelled bad. "See," she said accusingly, "I KNEW this internship thing would blow up!"

Jennifer felt a sense of despair. Should she work to shepherd Scott through to the end, or should she just call and tell him that it wasn't working and that he would have to make other arrangements?

6

CHILD COLLECTORS?

Lori D. Franklin

Pam Blakely, MSW, listened quietly as her colleagues discussed the Duncan family's home study.

"I think we should approve the home study," Christina Winters said. "This kid won't get other chances."

"But when will this stop?" Priya Kahn asked. "I mean, how many children will they want? Will we be discussing this again next year? Then again in 2012? I don't doubt their intentions, but we have to consider that this family might not realize their own capacity to care for children. I know it's an ugly term, and I hate to say it, but this family is starting to look like child collectors."

Development of this decision case was supported in part by the University of Oklahoma School of Social Work. It was prepared solely to provide material for class discussion and not to suggest either effective or ineffective handling of the situation depicted. Although the case is based on field research regarding an actual situation, names and certain facts may have been disguised to protect confidentiality. The author thanks the anonymous case reporter for cooperation in making this account available for the benefit of social work students and instructors.

"And with eight children in their home now, and so many already with special needs," Pam interjected, "are we really sure the Duncans are emotionally or financially prepared for a ninth child, especially a child with Down syndrome?"

The team was quiet, with their eyes on Pam.

"We might have different opinions about this," Pam offered to the team, "but, remember, we have to reach a consensus."

WORLD CHILD

World Child was a fifty-year-old nonprofit adoption agency in Lincoln, Nebraska, that provided a continuum of services from preadoption to postplacement. It was created in 1960 by a married couple who believed strongly that Jesus Christ had guided them to serve children at risk around the world. The agency was Christian based but did not require that adoptive families be Christian.

World Child maintained relationships with sister adoption agencies in China, Vietnam, India, South Korea, Haiti, and South Africa. Each year the agency placed approximately one hundred international children into adoptive homes in the United States. Most of the adoptive families participated in postplacement services that included summer camps and cultural events designed to keep children connected with their cultures of origin.

World Child was accredited by the Council on Accreditation, the national body that accredited many social service agencies, and was also a Hague-compliant provider. The Hague Convention on Protection of Children and Cooperation in Respect of Intercountry **Adoption**, initially drafted in 1993 but not fully enforced in the United States until 2008, was a significant treaty that regulated international adoptions to help reduce child trafficking. It was ratified by most, but not all, of the countries with which World Child worked. Many countries also required that home studies be performed by an agency that was trained and certified to assess in compliance with the Hague treaty. So World Child also provided home studies to families who were not pursuing placement through World Child but might be pursuing placement through non-Hague-compliant agencies or private services with legal counsel.

The agency was run by an executive director whose philosophy was very democratic and nonhierarchical. Team meetings were held to make important decisions, and every member had an equal say in the process. The team rotated who would facilitate the meetings, so there was one person in charge of keeping the group on track, but that person didn't have more power than any others. The team consisted of coordinators of each country's programs, all of whom were master's level clinicians, and a bachelor's level staff member from the Education Department. Then, various other staff members, such as case managers or home-study workers, would be invited to the meeting if there was a particular case that needed their input. This group evaluated families, with input from any other involved staff, and made crucial decisions about placements. But all team members had to reach an agreement. There was no voting process because the round-table discussion had to reach a consensus on how the agency would proceed. When opinions differed on an issue, decisions were slow and difficult to make, sometimes requiring long conversations to reach agreement.

ADOPTING INTERNATIONALLY

Families who came to World Child looking to adopt went through an exhaustive process. First, World Child provided an individual consultation and general written information on international adoptions and what to expect. Then it required they complete a two-part application and participate in two workshops. The first workshop focused on parent education and emphasized the special demands of international adoption. Prospective parents learned the importance of identifying the child's specific needs and ensuring they could meet those needs. The second workshop focused on the emotional issues stimulated by any adoption and more specifically by cross-cultural and cross-racial adoptions.

Prospective parents were often naive about the potential issues that tended to arise for adoptive children and families throughout their development. In the workshops, for example, staff discussed how people often said things such as, "God bless you, you are such a saint. You rescued that child from a life of poverty." The adopted kids tended to hear that kind of talk and would grow up thinking there was something wrong with them or their culture of origin and that they owed their adoptive parents something. Once parents went through the workshops, they were usually pretty comfortable saying, "No, that's not right, we didn't adopt our child for those reasons." Families who succeeded with international adoptions knew it wasn't about their being applauded and certainly not about "saving a child." It was about becoming a family.

Parents were sometimes interested in a particular country and were disappointed when they found out they didn't meet the criteria for that country. Other parents were open to considering children from any country, and they would meet with multiple country coordinators where they might qualify for placement. To adopt a child from South Korea, for instance, couples had to be married for at least three years and be twenty-five to forty-two years of age when they began the process. Unlike China, where prospective parents were disqualified if they were on medication for any mental health issues, South Korea required that mental illnesses be stable for five years and that parents provide documentation by a treating physician to prove mental stability. Korea had more in common with Westernized medicine and seemed to have an understanding of mental illness. However, it also had strict health requirements that often caused awkward problems for the staff at World Child. Most notable were the Korean requirements regarding body mass index, which were stricter than what was considered healthy by US standards. So prospective parents had to give health information on their intake applications, and Pam often had to tell a family that they were too overweight to be considered for a child from Korea.

The application process often took up to two years. Some countries required tours or residency in the country for a period of time before adoption, so these requirements added additional time, cost, and planning. After adoptive placement, World Child provided supportive services to help families with attachment and adjustment. World Child did not require participation in their regularly offered cultural programs or summer camps for adoptees, but it did strongly encourage such participation.

Then there was the matter of cost. International adoptions were expensive, and the coordinators had certainly heard snide comments from uneducated members of the public, such as "How much did you pay for that baby?" But there were costs, and parents had to be prepared for them. Most of these costs went directly to the sister agencies in the countries that were providing services for the children either in orphanages or in foster care. Potential parents were given a document that itemized every fee for each country, but most of the money went to assisting the sister agencies in providing care for the child and for humanitarian purposes within the birth country. The potential parents assumed the cost of care for any special medical or therapeutic needs of the child awaiting adoption while the child was in a foster care or orphanage setting. The fees were also needed to cover the various costs of processing immigration documents, translating documents, and paying in-country legal fees. World Child charged a fee for home studies as well as for postplacement services and case management. For example, adopting a baby from South Korea cost parents almost $30,000. This amount was pretty typical for most countries. Many families had to take out substantial loans that put their families at great financial risk.

COORDINATING ADOPTIONS

The coordinators had responsibility for working closely with agency staff from the country to which they were assigned, which involved communicating with the staff at the social service agencies in the birth countries that were arranging foster care, placing domestically, working with local adoption agencies, and overseeing orphanages. Because these agencies were typically understaffed, their staff members had numerous responsibilities. The coordinators communicated with them to find out about children available for adoption, then worked with the prospective adoptive families to coordinate home studies and preplacement education, and provided case management as the potential adoptive families went through the complicated legal process.

The children awaiting adoption experienced a wide variety of living conditions depending on their birth country. For example, most of the available adoptive children in South Korea were in foster care, but those in China and Russia were in orphanages. Although most Americans assumed these orphanages were filthy and inhumane, they actually were generally clean and provided adequate physical care, given the country's resources. The sister agencies that coordinated adoptive placements partnered with the orphanages to provide oversight and humanitarian aid to ensure the children received proper care. But the orphanages were typically understaffed, so caregivers were responsible for large numbers of children. As a result, children who came from orphanages were often withdrawn and showed signs of attachment difficulties. Although there were certainly cases of successful adults who had been raised in orphanages, there were more cases of children experiencing varying degrees of attachment problems.

PAM BLAKELY

Pam Blakely had worked with World Child for several years, originally doing fund-raising, then home studies and educational groups for prospective families. She commuted from Lincoln to the University of Nebraska at Omaha, working on her MSW while employed. Once she graduated, Pam was promoted to her current position as coordinator of Korean adoptions. Her job involved many complex diplomatic interactions with international as well as domestic systems of government and was often difficult and frustrating when barriers arose. But Pam firmly believed that every child deserved a family. She often stated that all the frustrations were worth it when a child came home.

She was naturally passionate about her work, especially because she herself was adopted in infancy from South Korea. Growing up as an internationally adopted child in the mostly white community of Lincoln, she was well aware of the difficulties the children she helped place might encounter. She and her older sister, Carolyn, had come to the United States together and were adopted by a white couple, Steve and Carol Blakely. Pam felt her childhood had been happy. The Blakelys gave the girls many opportunities, and Pam never doubted their love and care.

But Pam often wondered what life would have been like for her in the foster home where she and Carolyn had lived in Korea. She was especially thankful that her sister had not been raised in Korea. Carolyn was developmentally delayed and had multiple special needs. She still lived with the Blakelys and would probably not be able to live completely independently. Pam always knew while growing up that taking care of her sister was part of her role in the family and that her responsibilities for her sister would grow as their parents aged. She remembered a conversation with her fiancé, now her husband of three years, in which she had said, "Greg, before I can commit to building a life with you, I have to know that it's okay for my sister to come live with us someday. We will have to take care of her someday when my parents can't, and no matter what is happening with our lives at that time, she will be our responsibility." Greg had agreed and seemed to share her sense of loyalty to family. They were now expecting a baby. They had been exploring international adoption when Pam suddenly discovered she was expecting. They were nervous expectant parents but excited about the baby and their growing family.

THE DUNCANS

Marilyn and Bruce Duncan currently had eight children in their home, ranging from age two to seventeen. Only one child had been adopted through World Child, eight-year-old Colin. He had been placed almost six years earlier, when there were only two other children in the home. The other seven children were adopted domestically from state agencies or through private agencies and adoption attorneys. Marilyn homeschooled the children and arranged for their care. Bruce worked at Nebraska Plastics, a factory that made plastic connectors used in equipment for fences. He had worked there for three years, but about a year ago he had been laid off for approximately three months before being rehired. The factory was in Cozad, Nebraska, about a two-hour drive from Lincoln. The Duncans lived in a rural area just a few miles outside of Cozad.

The Duncans were Southern Baptists and were very involved in their church community. During the adoption process for Colin and in the other interactions with the family and the World Child staff that had followed, they had openly discussed that they felt it was their mission from God to help orphans and answer the call from children in need. They were committed to adoption and were eager to help children, especially children with special needs.

Maggie had been the first child to enter the Duncan's home, almost ten years earlier. Maggie was now twelve years old, Caucasian, and so severely and globally developmentally disabled that she was barely verbal and almost completely unable to care for herself. She was transported in a wheelchair and had a feeding tube and catheter. A home health nurse came to the home, but Marilyn Duncan was the primary provider of her minute-by-minute needs.

Next came Andrew, now seven and also Caucasian, who had been diagnosed with autism and required a great deal of care. He would frequently harm himself, banging his head against the wall and slamming his fists on the table. He made little eye contact and had very poor verbal skills. He often screamed when he became agitated, sometimes for more than an hour at a time. He had a case manager who came to the home weekly.

Then came the adoption with World Child and the placement of Colin. He was now eight and appeared to be doing well overall. As a child from India, his main opportunities for connection to his culture were through World Child's culture camps and events. The Duncans attended these events sometimes but had stated that they thought his connections to his Christian culture and his adoptive family were more important than his Indian culture. They worried he would become confused by learning about the different religions of India, so they did not attend any events that they feared would mention religion.

Colin had been in the home for almost two years when Grace arrived. Grace was now four, Caucasian, and had been adopted as an infant through a private adoption service. Her biological mother was fourteen when she had Grace and had sought placement for Grace as a newborn. Moreover, Grace was premature and had spent her first sixteen weeks in the neonatal intensive care unit. She was fed with a feeding tube for her first three weeks of life but had transitioned to a bottle without difficulty. She was underweight but appeared to be a healthy, happy child.

A few weeks after Grace's arrival, the Duncans adopted siblings, Matthew and Lauren. They had been pursuing adoptions privately and with the Child Protective Services Adoption Department simultaneously. Matthew was now fourteen, was African American, and had been diagnosed with learning disabilities. He read at a third-grade level. He didn't have friends and stated that he wasn't interested in making friends. He was adopted at age eleven, after spending more than seven years in foster care. His biological sister, Lauren, was now seventeen. She had also spent a long period of time in foster care, and the siblings had sometimes been together and sometimes apart in their foster placements. Lauren made Bs in school and had a new boyfriend. She helped some with the other children but also had a part-time job at the Country Grounds Coffeehouse in Cozad.

Last came Lakeisha and Jamal, African American birth siblings ages two and three, respectively. They were placed for adoption by Child Protective Services after their biological mother's rights were terminated when Lakeisha was only a few months old. Although Jamal was almost four, he was not yet toilet trained and had slurred speech that was difficult to understand. Lakeisha had tested positive for cocaine at birth and had been removed from her mother's custody immediately, but Jamal wasn't removed until after complaints of neglect. Both had been slow on developmental milestones. Lakeisha did not walk until age twenty-two months and still only used the words *mama* and *doggie*.

THE WAITING CHILD

Pam had just returned from lunch when she heard a message on her voice mail from Marilyn Duncan. Pam knew the Duncan family, primarily from their occasional participation in the World Child–sponsored cultural events related to India. Pam was not involved in providing their original adoption services and had only met them through their involvement in the postplacement services. They had, of course, worked more closely with Priya, who coordinated adoptions from India, so Pam was curious about why Marilyn had called her instead. She returned Marilyn's call.

"Hi, Marilyn," she began. "I got your message. What can I do for you?"

Marilyn launched into a story of a child from Thailand she had seen on the Internet. "She is the most beautiful child," Marilyn stated excitedly. "The minute I saw her, I knew that God was calling us to welcome her into our home."

Pam tried to think carefully before she spoke. She was a Christian, too, but often found herself feeling impatient with prospective parents who referenced Bible verses about saving orphans to explain why they wanted to adopt. She knew their intentions were good but thought it was part of her job to help people realize the true and often difficult realities of adoption. So Pam just listened a while longer.

"At church," Marilyn continued, "we had a sermon on adoption, and it was that very day that we saw her on the website. God asks us in James 1:27 to 'look after orphans and widows in their distress and to keep oneself from being polluted by the world. He will not leave you as orphans, He will come to you.' It was like all the pieces fit together, and we knew it was the right thing to do. She has Down syndrome, but we are just the perfect family for a special-needs child since we already have experience from raising Maggie and Andrew."

Finally, Marilyn got to the point. "We need someone to do a home study for us so that we can move forward with adopting her. I know you do the Korean program, but don't you know a lot about Thailand as well?"

"Are you wanting to adopt through World Child?" Pam hesitated. "We don't have a relationship with services in Thailand right now and don't do adoptions from there."

"No, no," Marilyn responded. "We are using another place this time."

"Oh, so can't they do a home study?" Pam asked. "I guess I'm not sure what you need from us right now."

"I hate to bother you, and I would have just had the social worker who did our other home studies do this one, too," Marilyn answered. "But for the international adoptions, the home study has to be done by a Hague-accredited agency. I already checked it out, and we really need you all to help us. Please. I know our family is big already, but I also know that we have enough love for more."

"I don't have expertise regarding Thailand, Marilyn," Pam replied. "I don't think any of us here does. I know the orphans from that part of the world have often been through a lot after the tsunami and the impact of AIDS. I really don't know about the living conditions for orphans there. I mean, do you know any of this child's history?"

"We are called to care for her. We will answer the call, and He will provide what we need to care for this little one," Marilyn responded with confidence.

"Marilyn," Pam said gently. "I'm going to have to take this to our team and get some input on this."

Pam sighed as she hung up the phone. She was aware of a strong feeling in herself that she already wanted to say no to this home study. But she would take it to the team.

DECISIONS ABOUT THE DUNCANS

The team met and quickly decided to secure consent from the Duncans to contact their previous caseworkers and home-study providers and to explore the situation further. They wanted to hear more about what had been happening with the family since the World Child placement and see if other providers had an opinion about the appropriateness of another adoption.

First, Pam called Alice Gaven, who had done the most recent home study for the placement of Lakeisha and Jamal.

"Yes, they asked me to do another home study for them, but I just didn't feel comfortable," Alice said. "I did the previous one, and although I really liked them and felt okay with the home study, I just know their situation and how hard it is with those special needs there already. Lakeisha and Jamal are a handful. And their finances are just pretty much paycheck to paycheck. Plus, this one is international, which is different for the home study. But I wouldn't have said yes anyway."

Next Pam called Melissa Mead, who had worked with the family for Grace's adoption.

"I can't believe they're wanting another child," Melissa stated flatly. "They're pushed to the max already. If we had known they were going to get other children so quickly after placing Grace, I'm not sure if we would have made the decisions we did at that time anyway. I've often wondered if Grace gets the attention she needs."

Pam felt she had her answer. Two professionals had agreed that the Duncans had their hands full.

She took this information to the team, ready to make the case that the agency should say no to the home study and encourage the Duncans to enjoy and appreciate the beautiful children they already had.

But before Pam made her report, Executive Director Meagan Bradley reported a series of phone calls from the family.

"I've had a number of calls from the Duncans," Meagan began. "They seem convinced that we are not going to do a home study for them and have really been relentless in trying to convince us to do one. Even though I told them I really didn't even know the specifics of this case, they continue to call."

For goodness' sake, Pam thought. *I never told them no, so they are just assuming that is what we will say. It's like they already know this isn't a good idea.*

"It started off with some pleading," Meagan related, "just to come by and see the house and visit. They said they would pay the home-study fee if we just came by and saw they were okay before we even decide about the home study. I told them that really isn't how we do it, and we wouldn't charge them a fee without truly providing the service. But she called back later, upset, saying, 'You are preventing God's plan for our family and for this poor little one.' I tried to calm her down and told her we would certainly discuss this and be as fair to her family as possible. But the conversation ended with her saying, 'This is God's plan for us, and we will pray and know that your hearts will be open. We're praying for you and your agency.'"

After some discussion, the team reached a consensus: in the spirit of giving all families a chance and not wanting to harm a relationship with a postadoption family that might need services in the future, they would send a worker out for a brief assessment. This worker would not be doing an official home study but would just assess the family in person so that better information would come back to the team from the family directly. Social worker Christina Winters, an experienced home study worker, was assigned this task.

CHRISTINA'S REPORT

Christina Winters made the two-hour journey to see the Duncans. Pam liked Christina and generally thought she did a good job with home studies. She had worked with the agency much longer than Pam and was a licensed clinical social worker. Pam also knew that Christina had spiritual beliefs similar to the Duncans', but she believed Christina had good judgment and certainly was aware that multiple adoptions were not for everyone.

The team met again on Tuesday morning, one week later. Christina opened the discussion by reporting that she had conducted a home-study interview with the Duncan family and had started their official home study.

"Wait a minute," Pam began. "I thought we were just assessing them further?"

"Well," Christina answered, "they live two hours from here. I got out there and met with them, and they really won me over, I guess. They are strapped financially, but they have backups in place. The dad is pretty employable, and they really do seem to know how to manage their money well enough to keep things going. The house is clean, the kids seem happy, everyone is well cared for. I just couldn't see a reason not to go ahead and start the study while I was out there. Especially since just having a home study done doesn't mean the agency has approved it."

"Does it imply to the family that we are supporting them, though?" Pam wondered out loud.

"That's true, it might." said Margot Nickels, the coordinator of Chinese adoptions. "I guess our decision now is if we approve this as saying that World Child recommends this family for placement. We can still say we don't approve this study to go forward."

"What about our concerns we discussed last time, though, Christina?" Elizabeth Caney, the coordinator of Vietnamese adoptions, asked. "You know, about what will happen with the kids with special needs after the parents pass away? Did they seem aware of all of that?"

"I pulled aside the older kids and talked with them alone," Christina said. "They really seemed to understand, and they said they were just as devoted to their family as their parents are. They are very spiritual also and were able to articulate that this is part of God's plan for them as well. Lauren especially already helps with the children and said she feels responsible for them. She is a very mature young woman."

"I believe that," Pam began. "I believe they are 100 percent genuine in saying they will take care of this child forever, but they just don't know what that really means. We just have to remember that adoption triad here. We always try to consider the birth mother's perspective, the adoptive family's perspective, and the child's perspective. So if I were the birth mother, would I want my child going to this family? I just don't know if they can take on my child with all they have going on."

"But, Pam," Christina responded, "if you were the child, would you rather be raised in an orphanage or have a family, even if it's chaotic?"

"I know, I know," Pam said. "I don't know the answer. But I know that her needs as a child with Down syndrome are sometimes more than an orphanage can handle." Pam felt tears start to well up as she spoke.

"I think we should approve the home study," Christina Winters said. "This kid won't get other chances."

"But when will this stop?" Priya Kahn asked. "I mean, how many children will they want? Will we be discussing this again next year? Then again in 2012? I don't doubt their intentions, but we have to consider that this family might not realize their own capacity to care for children. I know it's an ugly term, and I hate to say it, but this family is starting to look like 'child collectors.'"

"And with eight children in their home now, and so many of them with special needs," Pam interjected, "are we really sure the Duncans are emotionally or financially prepared for a ninth child, especially a child with Down syndrome?"

The team was quiet, with their eyes on Pam.

"We all might have different opinions about this," Pam offered to the team. "But, remember, we have to reach a consensus."

Pam wasn't sure what she thought anymore. She didn't really have a sense for what the rest of the team thought either. She knew they could ask the family to do any number of things to complete a plan, but she just wasn't sure what kind of plan would make her feel comfortable with this family's assuming responsibility for a ninth child. And Christina was right. There weren't many parents lining up to adopt children with Down syndrome. But the team had to reach a consensus, and Pam's input was as valuable as every other member of the team.

What is the right thing to do? She wondered. *And how can we reach a consensus about this family?*

7

I'M A SOCIAL WORKER!

Karen A. Gray and Julie Sprinkle

In 2000, when new MSW graduate Kiona Baker accepted a social work position with the Florence County (South Carolina) school system to work in the Supporting Good Behavior Program, she thought that she would finally be able to do what she loved: help children discover their talents and achieve their goals. But over the next four months, her excitement became a distant memory. With limited access to resources and little support by her colleagues, her main feeling was frustration. By December, she concluded that her classroom was simply a dumping ground. Something inside her finally snapped when the principal sent an in-school suspension (ISS) student to Kiona's class because the ISS

Development of this decision case was supported in part by the University of South Carolina College of Social Work. It was prepared solely to provide material for class discussion and not to suggest either effective or ineffective handling of the situation depicted. Although the case is based on field research regarding an actual situation, names and certain facts may have been disguised to protect confidentiality. The authors thank the anonymous case reporter for cooperation in making this account available for the benefit of social work students and instructors.

classroom was full. *Am I really helping anyone here?* Kiona wondered. *I want to help these children, but I don't have the resources I need to do so. Now what?!*

THE SUPPORTING GOOD BEHAVIOR PROGRAM

The Supporting Good Behavior Program (SGBP) originated in Charleston County, and then officials in Florence County decided to replicate it. It was a grant-funded program designed for high school students who had been in alternative schools or homeschooled due to chronic, severe behavior problems. The goal of the program, which was housed in regular high schools, was to modify disruptive or inappropriate student behaviors so that the students could be mainstreamed in regular classrooms; students were to be in the special SGBP classroom for a few periods each day and in "regular" classrooms the rest of the day for six to eight weeks. SGBP was funded for only one year. If not successful, it would not receive further funding.

LAKE CITY HIGH

Florence County, South Carolina, was politically conservative and deeply religious. There were approximately thirty thousand children in the Florence County school system. SGBP was housed in Lake City High School (LCHS), located in a working-class town with slightly more African American students than Caucasian. Most of the families had lived in the area for years. In fact, some of the teachers at LCHS had taught the parents of their current students.

KIONA AND HER JOB

Kiona Baker received her MSW in the spring of 2000. A young, African American woman, she was bright and hard working. She had high expectations for herself and pushed herself to meet those expectations. Kiona's social work experiences were based mostly in mental health.

During her field placement in Georgia for her bachelor's in social work, she had worked at a group home for troubled youth. Her MSW placement had been at a Veterans Administration Hospital. Besides these internships, Kiona also had paid social work experience. Between graduating and entering the advanced standing program at the University of South Carolina College of Social Work, she had worked for ten months on a psychiatric unit with children and adults. She had realized that she enjoyed working with children, even the difficult ones. While attending the MSW program, she decided she wanted to work exclusively with children.

Kiona had grown up in a county close to Florence that was predominately African American, rural, and poor. She felt drawn to children with behavior problems because she remembered her own problems as a child. Although never labeled or referred for help, Kiona had had "problems with authority figures." She thought that she had learned to overcome those feelings, and she wanted to work with children to help them cope better and correct their behaviors.

Kiona received her MSW two weeks prior to accepting her position with the Florence County school system. The county didn't seem to mind that she wasn't licensed as an MSW yet. She was the new SGBP's first and only employee, and her job was to modify the children's behavior so that they could return to regular classrooms.

COLLEAGUES

Paula Nelson, an older white woman, was a clinician in private practice and Kiona's clinical supervisor. She tried to meet with Kiona once each week for consultation and debriefing in her office, but her schedule was sometimes so hectic that she had to cancel the meetings. When she and Kiona did meet, she was supportive and understanding of the difficulties Kiona faced.

Tom Mitchell was Kiona's assistant. Tom was a thirty-six-year-old African American man recently laid off from a job in the banking industry. He was supposed to help Kiona with instruction, supervision, and behavior management, but he had neither experience nor training in working with children. A former college football player, he was also supposed to serve as a good role model for the students. But when he wasn't reading the newspaper, he often caused problems by displaying an antagonistic and disrespectful attitude toward the students.

Tom and Kiona were among the youngest employees at LCHS. Almost all of the teachers were older than fifty. Only ten of the eighty teachers were African American, and more than 30 percent of them were new to the school.

Preston Maxwell was the principal at LCHS and Kiona's supervisor. A middle-aged white man, Preston had multiple roles and responsibilities in the school and the larger community. Although Kiona rarely spoke with him, she thought he felt passionately about students, and she considered him to be a fair man. Several teachers praised him for the opportunities he tried to provide to all students. With the "No Child Left Behind" laws, he had to attend many meetings off school grounds. There was also talk about turning LCHS into a vocational magnet school for the county, which required many other meetings.

GREAT EXPECTATIONS

Kiona reported to work on July 31, with classes scheduled to begin on August 14. On August 2, Preston told Kiona, "We'll screen the kids one at a time. This will help us determine who's most likely to succeed in the new SGBP program. You'll receive computers with educational software, NovaNet, that will teach the students their required educational components while you work with them on behavior modification and social skills training."

Using NovaNet made Kiona indirectly responsible for administering instructional materials to the students. This made her slightly nervous, but she knew the students would be in "regular" classrooms most of the day, and after six weeks they would be promoted to regular classrooms full-time, so she decided the computers might not be too bad a substitute for a live teacher.

Beginning August 3, Kiona attended four days of new school employee trainings, cleared her classroom of old furniture and books, set up her classroom, and prepared to screen prospective students.

By August 9, she started getting nervous that students had not been screened yet. But she was so new, both to the job and to the profession, that she was afraid to say anything. Plus, she trusted Preston to do as he'd said. But Preston instead unilaterally assigned the students on August 11. By that date, he still had not followed through on his promise of computers. Kiona received many hand-me-down materials, such as reading and math books, but no guidelines or curriculum for the social skills training and behavior modification that she had been hired to do. The only explanation Preston gave Kiona was, "This is a new program, and we just can't have everything in place by the beginning of the year." Kiona suspected the problem was actually a matter of poor planning.

Staff members who knew the children Preston assigned to Kiona's classroom briefed her about their behavior. For example, one teacher told Kiona, "Chuck Duke—I can't believe he's not in jail. Chip Andrews—he has three counts breaking and entering. Jamie Jones hasn't been in regular classroom since he was in the fifth grade. And Mike Moss, well, he's been in an alternative school since he was in the fifth grade." Kiona concluded, "I pretty much got the students nobody else wanted." And they were placed in her classroom for up to three periods per day.

AND CLASSES BEGIN

On August 22, at her first weekly meeting with her supervisor, Paula Nelson, Kiona reflected on her first day with the students. "When classes began," Kiona stated, "the students thought that they were going to be in regular classrooms. They did not understand why they were placed in a restricted setting. Preston tried to explain to the group that they were in a transition class where they would be somewhat self-contained until they earned their way out. After hearing this, they exploded! To them, 'self-contained' is like kindergarten because they have to be escorted everywhere. They demanded to be taken out of the class."

Kiona continued, "The students were cussing, ranting, and raving. For the first few hours, I just had to let them vent. The boys had records of attacking teachers, so I definitely was not going to be very confrontational with them! I never felt as if I was about to be attacked, except for Jamie, but he has a one-to-one child behavior specialist, a worker from mental health who must be with him at all times because he can be violent. After the students calmed down, I let them know that they weren't in prison. Then I tried to explain the program to them again: 'The alternative settings that you've been in, like homebound placement or the Florence District Alternative School, are set up a lot differently than regular school. This program is designed to help you transition back into regular classes. We just want you to be successful in your high school careers and this program will help you do that.'"

GETTING TO KNOW HER STUDENTS

A few days later Kiona relayed to Paula, "After being with the boys for up to three periods every day, I have formed my own opinions and impressions of them. In some ways, my assessments are similar to those of the other teachers, but in some ways they are very different." She had originally had several other students, but they had dropped out within the first month of school. Kiona described her continuing students:

Mike Moss: Mike was a slender, five-foot eight-inch, African American male with a lisp and a short fade hairdo. He was fifteen years old. Mike had a great sense of humor, yet he could also become very angry in a matter of seconds. He had to be reminded often to refrain from using foul language. He had numerous behavioral and emotional problems. According to his school records, he was labeled EMD (educable mentally disabled), EMH (educable mentally handicapped), and BED (behaviorally emotionally disabled). When he was about nine years old, he was screened by a mental health provider and sent to anger-management classes. He was also prescribed Ritalin for ADHD (attention deficit hyperactivity disorder). However, Mike didn't want to participate in the anger-management courses or take the medication, and his mother didn't force him. His teachers had considered him a "problem" student since he was in the third grade.

Mike was placed in an alternative setting because he refused to do his work, fought with teachers, would not stay on task, and instigated numerous fights. He reacted bitterly to being placed in SGBP. He had been in an alternative school for four years. He said that he had earned his way out of Florence District Alternative School and wanted to know why he had to come through the SGBP to transition into regular classes. Mike thought that he was unfairly picked for the program and claimed, "There were other kids from the Alternative School who weren't placed in this program. Why was I?"

Chuck Dukes: Chuck was an eighteen-year-old, dark-skinned African American who liked to wear flashy clothes. He was slender and at least six feet two inches, with short hair and a mustache. Chuck could be very friendly, but more often than not he was obnoxious. He did a great deal of repetitive singing and dancing; he would just get up from his seat and start dancing. He was polite, but only if you're weren't trying to be an authority figure with him or give him any directives. Chuck had never been referred to mental health.

Chuck was placed in an alternative setting because he inappropriately touched girls, refused to do his work, and talked back to his teachers. When Chuck discovered that he was in SGBP, he felt as if he had been lied to. He said, "I would rather be homebound than be in here." He believed that he was placed in the program because he was black and because the teachers didn't like him.

Jamie Jones: Jamie was a five-foot seven-inch, fifteen-year-old Caucasian with red hair. He was slightly overweight, had acne, and didn't dress very well because his family had little money. Jamie could be extremely defensive. He was frightening when he had an explosive episode.

Jamie was labeled EMD, EMH, and BED and had a history of depression. He visited a therapist on a regular basis. Jamie's grandparents were having an MRI and a CAT scan performed on him to determine if there were anything physically wrong with him.

Jamie's grandmother said that he had been placed in an alternative setting because he needed a speech pathologist to help him. So the administrators had placed him in a special class with children who had emotional or behavioral disabilities or both. Jamie had attacked a teacher. His grandmother said, "He was just acting like the other students." Jamie came to LCHS from a day-treatment program. According to his child behavior specialist, his treatment team did not think that he needed SGBP and wanted him to be transitioned immediately into a classroom.

Alex Mitchell: Alex was a five-foot five-inch African American male with short hair. Kiona said, "He was unbelievably obnoxious. You had to work hard to get along with him. Alex was very rude and disrespectful. He seemed angry all the time. I never saw Alex be nice to anyone, not even the other students."

Keith Patton: Keith was a seventeen-year-old Caucasian. He was six feet five inches tall and very thin. He usually wore baggy jeans, oversize clothes, and a great deal of jewelry. He had a "gentlemanly" personality and answered questions with "yes, ma'am" and "no, ma'am."

Chip Andrews: Chip was a sixteen-year-old white male. He was approximately six feet one inch tall and weighed about 220 pounds. He was always respectful. Kiona said, "You have to get on him about his language, but he is probably the best-behaved student in the class." He had been in a therapeutic group home for thirteen months. But Chip's behavior had improved to the point that he was returned to his guardian's care. He had been placed in SGBP because of his disruptive classroom behavior. Kiona said, "His ADHD was so bad that I could tell when he had not taken his medication."

THESE ARE MY RESOURCES?

Many of the materials that the school provided to Kiona were inappropriate for her students because the material required basic reading and thinking skills, but they could barely read and write. Some students' IQs were so low that they were considered mildly mentally retarded. Mike's IQ was sixty-five, and Jamie's was in the high fifties. In reading, Mike struggled with words such as *cat* and *permit*. Jamie could write his name but could not recognize any other words. Chuck and Chip could read a little bit better, but both of them were considered learning disabled in written expression. In fact, all of the children had been tested and diagnosed as learning disabled.

In addition to inadequate materials, Kiona struggled with limited family involvement. None of the parents contacted her, so it was up to her to track them down. She was usually unable to get in touch with the boys' parents via telephone or mail. She occasionally spoke with Jamie's mother and grandmother because they were part of his crisis plan. If he started acting out, Kiona was supposed to call his grandmother and let her speak to him, which was supposed to calm him down. Kiona never met Mike's mother. She spoke to her once on the phone, but Mike's mother said she couldn't meet with Kiona because she didn't have any transportation. Kiona met with Chuck's mother only twice, even though she drove a bus for the school. As for Chip, Kiona met his grandmother once during an Individualized Education Program (IEP) meeting. Kiona received little support or assistance from the students' families as a whole.

The promised computers did not arrive until September 11, and the students were not trained to use them until September 15.

As she struggled with the SGBP, Kiona worried about what she was accomplishing. To make matters worse, Preston was busy and hard to find. She began to ask herself, *Do I really want this job? Is this what I set out to do? There's no way I can teach these boys this stuff. In South Carolina, I'm not even allowed to teach instructional material. I'm nervous about doing a good job, especially since continued funding depends on it!* When she did have opportunity to confide her fears to Preston, he simply responded, "Don't worry about it."

IS THIS PROGRESS?

By October, as the SGBP deteriorated, Kiona felt increasingly frustrated. Despite a strong desire to help the children, she had limited resources and little support.

During her weekly consultation with Paula, Kiona lamented, "SGBP is supposed to be a social skills program with group materials that would teach the students about aggressive, assertive, and passive behaviors. But the material is too difficult for the students to read and comprehend on their own. Yet when I break the lesson down and started explaining things to them, it is too simple, and they become rowdy. In the end, I have to put the lesson aside, deal with their present behavior, and give them the same old speech about why they are in this classroom."

To illustrate, Kiona relayed the following story to Paula. "I was trying to teach the students about what good classroom behavior looks like.

"Chuck says, 'Why do we have to do this all the time?! Why do we always have to talk about behavior?! This is stupid.' Mike added, 'My momma taught me right from wrong. We ain't dumb. They're treating us like babies. We just don't want to do this stuff.'

"Of course, I'm covering up the language. My students use a lot of expletives. Mike and Chuck got the rest of the class so upset that I had to put the lesson off to the side to keep the situation from getting ugly. I told them, 'Nobody thinks you're dumb. I know your mom taught you right and wrong. But this is the curriculum that has been provided for me, and I have to follow it. I understand how you feel, but I have a job to do.'

"But they asked, again, 'Why do we always talk about behavior? This is getting old. I'm tired of talking about this. We talk about this all day long.'

"I tried to be therapeutic by letting them vent, but trying to reason with them was like talking to a wall!"

Kiona continued, "Adding to their frustration is the fact that they were only supposed to be in the class for six weeks and then transition back into regular classes for the periods that I have them. Since they're now in their seventh week with me, they have quite discouraged. Several of the boys have made comments like 'I'm never going to get out of here, so I give up. I'm not even going to try anymore.'

DESPERATELY SEEKING STAFF SUPPORT

Kiona didn't think that this situation was fair to her students. When she finally caught up with Preston, she told him, "My boys need a timeline, a goal to work toward, something to motivate them."

"We don't owe them a time frame," Preston responded. "They will get out when they have earned their way out." Kiona did not understand what that meant.

The teachers at the school compounded Kiona's difficulties. They expected her to teach. They didn't seem to understand that she was a social worker, not a teacher. Since the hall phone was in her room, the other teachers were always coming in and out. The majority of the teachers at the school were women older than fifty who didn't hesitate to share their opinion that Kiona's students were "all going to end up in the state hospital."

Kiona quickly discovered that play therapy was useful with her students. With all the teachers coming in and out of her class, however, it was soon all over school that "Kiona doesn't do anything with those kids! She just plays cards with them. She's so lazy; she doesn't even try to teach them anything!" This frustrated Kiona, but she didn't know how to approach the teachers to explain her job and skills.

Kiona's assistant Tom unfortunately had the ability to make any given situation worse. He frequently antagonized the students. When Chuck proclaimed, "You can't tell me what to do; you're not my daddy," Tom replied, "If I were your daddy, you wouldn't be like you are now. How much can your momma care about you? She has an eighteen-year-old son who doesn't know how to read." Kiona had to run interference between Tom and the students on a regular basis.

In addition to the difficulties with her assistant and teachers at the high school, Kiona received limited support from her boss. Preston admitted that he was not very accessible. In fact, he was rarely in his office. When Kiona did finally track him down, she said, "I don't feel like I have any support around here. It seems like I'm fighting an uphill battle that gets steeper every day."

"Don't worry about it," Preston replied. "We're flying the plane as we're building it, so encountering some difficulties is only natural. It'll all work out in the end. You'll see."

When Kiona related her troubles to her clinical supervisor, Paula advised, "You're doing what you know to do. The school knew that you were an MSW, not a certified teacher, when they hired you."

"I know you're right," Kiona said, "but I just get so upset and anxious sometimes. I really feel for these boys. The system has let them down in so many ways, and I don't want to be one more person in that system to let them down. Yet it feels as if I am. I've been in this job for only a few months, and I feel like quitting already, but I can't afford to financially or professionally."

"You do seem unhappy," Paula responded, "and the more you talk about your job, the more it sounds like you're in over your head. But in the end only you can decide if you should stay with SGBP or resign."

In November, Preston decided that students from regular classrooms would come into Kiona's classroom to learn how to use the NovaNet educational software. Learning how to use the program would enable these students to meet the goals on their IEP's. Kiona had the new students for three weeks at a time. They were exposed to the NovaNet program and then they would leave. Scheduling who got on the computers, when, and for how long became difficult for Kiona to work out. The students from SGBP became very territorial. They cussed out the NovaNet students for sitting in "their" seats and constantly asked Kiona, "Why are they leaving? Why can't we leave, too?" Then Kiona had to explain to her students, again, why they were in SGBP.

Kiona's dissatisfaction escalated throughout the semester. Besides having the behavior-modification students and the problem students from other classes who needed NovaNet training to meet their IEP goals, in December the school started using Kiona's classroom for ISS. No one informed Kiona that her class would be used as an ISS annex. Instead, the principal simply sent an ISS student to her class. When the first unknown student walked in, Kiona asked, "Can I help you?" The student responded, "ISS is full, so they're putting me down here for two days."

At that moment, something inside Kiona snapped. She had had enough. *Am I really helping anyone here?* Kiona wondered. *I want to help these children, but I don't have the resources I need to do so. Now what?!*

8

FLYING FLAGS IN ALABAMA

Noël Busch-Armendariz, Dawnovise N. Fowler,
and Terry A. Wolfer

Social worker Jean Gibson, a site coordinator at the Center for Children and Families, received a positive and glowing performance evaluation. Program managers Lisa Hughes and Kelly Parker exclaimed, in both oral and written reports, that she was doing an "awesome job."

Arriving at the office one week later, Jean received a voicemail from Lisa: "Call me right away when you get in." But aware of how much she had to get done that morning, Jean decided, *I'll catch up with her at our regular one o'clock meeting this afternoon.*

At 11:30 AM, Lisa called Jean again. This time Jean answered the phone. "When I leave you a message," Lisa said vehemently, "I expect you to call me back right away."

Development of this decision case was supported in part by the University of Texas—Austin School of Social Work. It was prepared solely to provide material for class discussion and not to suggest either effective or ineffective handling of the situation depicted. Although the case is based on field research regarding an actual situation, names and certain facts may have been disguised to protect confidentiality. The authors thank the anonymous case reporter for cooperation in making this account available for the benefit of social work students and instructors.

"Oh," Jean responded, "I didn't realize it was so urgent. I've been really busy and just thought it could wait until our one o'clock meeting. Then we can discuss it in person. What's going on?"

"I need to talk to you about Melissa and the flags."

"Melissa and the flags?" Jean repeated, puzzled.

"Yes, and at this point," Lisa said abruptly, "we'll just talk about it at one."

What was that about? Jean wondered after hanging up. *She sounded pretty upset. Did I hurt Melissa's feelings? But what's the big deal?*

HIGHLAND CENTER

Highland Center, a large nonprofit mental health agency, was contracted by the Alabama Department of Mental Health and Developmental Disabilities (MHDD) to provide inpatient and outpatient services to the indigent, mentally ill population of Huntsville and the surrounding area. However, services were woefully underfunded, and in an effort to bring attention to the seriousness of the problems that Highland's Crisis Center faced the center's clinicians used the local newspaper to publicize the inadequate funding and substandard services that resulted. They pointed media attention, for example, to fourteen-hour wait times for clients, client admissions without available beds, and clients having to sleep on couches. With this negative publicity, Highland challenged MHDD to increase the state's allocations, noting especially that Highland provided services for 19 percent of the state's indigent mentally ill but received only 7 percent of the state's mental health budget.

When MHDD rejected Highland's request, Highland administrators decided they could not sustain adequate services for this population and decided to stop altogether. They instructed clinicians to terminate with their clients within two weeks but provided little more communication about these drastic programmatic changes. Agency staff suffered the uncertain future of their jobs and their clients. During a three-day period, cases for a total of three thousand mentally ill clients were terminated and transitioned to three other mental health agencies in the area. The three agencies that received Highland's caseload were Consortium of Therapeutic Services, Pineview Mental Health, and Center for Children and Families. The cases and corresponding funding were distributed equally among them.

CENTER FOR CHILDREN AND FAMILIES

Of the three agencies that absorbed Highland's caseload, the Center for Children and Families (CCF) was the only one not originally developed as a community mental health agency. Instead, it had begun as a private agency that offered counseling to families and children and school-based services. Despite no previous experience serving severely mentally ill (SMI) clients, CCF rapidly geared up by hiring staff and developing programs and services in order to accommodate Highland's clients. There was no other place for this population to receive crisis services. A local homeless shelter initially donated extra space to the CCF. Later, when Pineview Mental Health closed its doors, CCF acquired its building and assumed its client caseload as well.

The CCF's upper administration—a chief executive officer and a program director—depended on midlevel managers to oversee programs and program staff. Although the agency pieced together program funding, it had ample staff at the midmanagement level. Both Lisa Hughes and Kelly Parker had been midlevel managers of children's programs at CCF for many years before the agency decided to take on mental health services. They became codirectors of CCF's mental health services. Kelly coordinated case managers, and Lisa coordinated therapists, but their management roles at CCF were not easily distinguishable. There was little interaction between upper-level administrators and program staff. Lisa and Kelly seemed to work as a team, even sharing an office at the CCF administrative building. Both were attractive, vibrant women in their early thirties and usually dressed in business attire with suits and high heels. Both had earned master degrees in human relations. Lisa also earned her license in professional counseling and had previous work experience with children. Although they always worked as a team, six-foot Lisa had a more commanding presence, led the staff meetings, and did most of the talking. Kelly, in contrast, often nodded and primarily spoke in agreement with Lisa.

When CCF took on the SMI clients, it hired support staff to focus on the clerical and billing demands. A white woman in her fifties, Norma Tisdale was the office manager for the new satellite office. She was politically and personally conservative. Her son was serving with the military in Iraq, and she kept his military photo on her desk. She, along with several other coworkers, decorated her desk with religious plaques and items and used Bible verses as screen savers. When Norma relocated to the main office to assist the program managers with the demands of the expansion, Melissa Draper was hired to take her place. Melissa was in her late twenties and petite, with short dark hair and freckles. She tended to look stern but was friendly when she spoke. She was married and had recently bought a house in the suburbs.

JEAN GIBSON

A native of Alabama, Jean Gibson had received her MSW from the University of Alabama. A twenty-eight-year-old lesbian, she was in a long-term committed relationship. As a therapist at Highland, she saw the writing on the wall once Highland decided to stop taking state funding and serving the mentally ill. She quickly decided to look for other employment. She was particularly interested in obtaining a position with an agency where she could continue to use and develop her clinical skills with SMI clients and that had good health benefits. Because Jean and her partner had decided to pursue donor insemination so Jean could become a biological parent, Jean considered health coverage important for herself and her future children. She received job offers from all three take-over agencies and eventually accepted a position as therapist at CCF. She liked the "positive energy" at CCF and its "home-based" approach to serving its clients. During her initial interview, Jean got the sense that at CCF she and her clients would have a much different experience than at Highland. Staff members at Highland had low energy and were experiencing burnout, whereas staff members at CCF seemed flexible and open. Jean initially thought that she shared many commonalities with the CCF agency and its staff. Coworkers described her as competent, thorough, and "a worker bee" with a low-key approach. Although she usually had an opinion on important issues, she was soft-spoken.

To receive donor insemination, Jean had to travel more than ninety minutes for treatment in Chattanooga, Tennessee, because she could not find any fertility specialists who provided services to lesbian couples in Huntsville. There was never any resistance from Lisa or Kelly when Jean needed to attend her fertility treatment appointments. In fact, a couple of times during her initial months of employment at CCF, Jean had to postpone meetings with Lisa and Kelly or reschedule client appointments so that she could make the commute to receive treatment. They were always supportive of her, and Jean was grateful. Within several months, Jean was pregnant with her first child. Although she appreciated being accommodated, she also noticed that colleagues at CCF seldom asked about her partner or offered support for this endeavor. She did not hide that she was lesbian, but she also did not talk much about her family at work, and she knew not to talk to Norma about her personal life. Unlike the others, however, Melissa asked questions about Jean's pregnancy that Jean was willing to answer.

After eighteen months as a therapist with CCF, Lisa and Kelly offered Jean a promotion. She would now serve in the position of site coordinator over the newly expanded program units that CCF housed in Pineview's old space. Although excited by the prospect of additional responsibility and professional growth opportunities, Jean had some concerns about taking this position. Foremost was the lack of a clear job description. Her supervisors, Lisa and Kelly, often referred to her position interchangeably as "site coordinator," "clinical supervisor," and "site supervisor." Even when Jean pressed, she could not get a clear answer on her responsibilities but attributed this lack of initial planning to the hectic transition period. What was clear to Jean was that both supervisors were very enthusiastic about promoting her. Because the position was new, and CCF was still new at serving SMI clients, Lisa and Kelly asked Jean to develop her own job description.

In her new position, Jean provided a mix of supervisory and clinical services. In all, she supervised four case managers, a day treatment counselor, an office manager, and a receptionist, and she coordinated several psychiatrists' schedules. In total, she was providing clinical supervision for program staff that saw about 240 clients. In addition, she herself provided therapy for about 10 clients, all of whom also had a case manager, as well as backup "crisis services" for case managers. For example, if a client was suicidal, Jean would conduct an assessment and determine the next course of intervention. She also conducted two outpatient therapy groups.

Before accepting the promotion, Jean had several concerns. Because she had just recently received her license in clinical social work, she lacked experience supervising other clinicians, professionals, and administrative support staff. She had little preparation or training for her new administrative role. Furthermore, she *did not trust* the program director (Lisa and Kelly's supervisor) because the woman had little clinical experience and expertise. One time, when Jean had staffed a case with her, the director had said, "Well, people have the right to commit suicide if they want to." Jean was also concerned that she would have difficulty balancing these new responsibilities and parenting. Although she expressed these concerns to Lisa and Kelly, the position excited her. It would be her first opportunity to gain such skills and experience. Lisa and Kelly seemed to understand the importance of motherhood to Jean. Lisa had also been pursuing motherhood and had recently been pregnant, but she had miscarried. They were very supportive of her professional concerns and personal goals and encouraged her to take the position at Pineview.

JEAN'S GROUP

Soon after beginning to lead the therapy groups, Jean realized that the group room did not have a clock. She asked receptionist Amanda Moore to purchase a clock for the group room, and Amanda suggested that they ask the Lexapro sales representative. "They will probably give us a clock since [staff psychiatrist] Dr. Ash is one of the top prescribers of Lexapro in Alabama."

"Well," Jean responded, "that explains why we have all the Lexapro stuff around the office. Great, let's ask them for a clock."

The clients in one of Jean's groups had a long history with each other. They had received mental health services from the two mental health agencies that occupied the building before Pineview.

To Jean, it seemed that the group had "an old drinkin' buddy feel," and she was the outsider being introduced to the longstanding members. The group comprised three men—Brian, David, and John—and one woman—Kathy. All of the members except John always contributed to the group discussions.

Over the first several weeks that Jean facilitated the group, she made special attempts to engage John in the group process because he was very quiet. His affect was consistently flat, and he was not easy to engage, but he attended regularly. When she first met him, she had thought, *He seems isolated and unkempt.* He was a big red-haired guy who wore heavy-metal T-shirts.

One week, when on a routine visit with the site psychiatrist, Dr. Williams, John said that he was suicidal. When that happened, Dr. Williams left John in her office and asked Jean to further assess him for suicidality. Jean got the sense from Dr. Williams that the doctor was uncomfortable with John. *She acts like she's afraid of him,* Jean observed. Jean assumed she had been called in because she had the most experience with John and suicidal clients. When Jean talked with him, John acknowledged he had guns in his house but said he would not kill himself because he had a wife and a daughter. Jean had not known John long, so she was trying to determine his baseline. As they talked, Jean wondered, *Is he a real threat to himself and perhaps others? Is he at real risk for suicide today, more than other days that he has come to group?*

Although Dr. Williams asked for Jean's professional judgment, she did not consult Jean when deciding to call 911. Dr. Williams simply informed Jean of her decision, and Jean told John what Dr. Williams was doing. Jean asked him to wait until emergency services came to help them sort through what was going on with him, but John refused and left abruptly.

Concerned about John's well-being, Jean tried to contact him. That's when she discovered that the phone number listed in his chart was disconnected and the mailing address did not include a street name and number, only a rural route. When she checked with the police, they didn't know how to locate him either. *Will he ever show up to group again?* Jean worried. *This agency is SO uncomfortable with suicidal clients.*

In fact, John missed group for only one week and then returned as usual.

"I'm so glad you're here," Jean greeted John, trying not to sound too relieved that he was back. *I better not make a big deal out of his return.*

For the first time, John began to talk in the group. He talked about his combat experiences in Desert Storm, his nightmares, and how he wanted to kill himself because he couldn't get certain thoughts out of his head.

Oh, he's a war veteran, Jean realized, *he should be getting services from the Veterans Administration. Should I keep that information to myself? Because our clinic is for people who do not have other resources, he might be transferred to the Veterans Administration for services.* She saw John's suicide risk even more clearly now that she understood his history of traumatic events.

The other members of the group—Brian, David, and Kathy—also contributed to the discussion about how war affects people. The group discussed the invasion of Iraq and how this affected veterans and their families. In general, the group was disturbed by the country's support of war. The group sentiment was, "How can some people glorify war? The grim reality is that war hurts people." Jean moved the group to thinking about how to respond when others "cheerlead" for war. In the end, she was satisfied with how the session ended and thought, *That was a good group because John participated.*

As Jean left the group room following the session, Melissa approached her. "Jean, look at these! I found them at the Dollar Store." While the group was in session, she had decorated all of the reception area, including the end tables, her desk, and the front door with American flags. She had also draped Fourth of July ribbons across the desk and hung a large banner across the doorway that read "God Bless America."

"Melissa," Jean ventured, "I don't think this is appropriate, you know. This could be bothersome for some people. I think that we should take these down."

"I didn't know someone might not like patriotism," Melissa said, surprised, and then walked away.

When Jean arrived at the office the next morning, she had a voicemail from Lisa: "Call me right away when you get in." But aware of how much she had to get done that morning, Jean decided, *I'll catch up with her at our regular one o'clock meeting this afternoon.*

At 11:30 AM, Lisa called Jean again. This time Jean answered the phone. "When I leave you a message," Lisa said vehemently, "I expect you to call me back right away."

"Oh," Jean responded, "I didn't realize it was so urgent. I've been really busy and just thought it could wait until our one o'clock meeting. Then we can discuss it in person. What's going on?"

"I need to talk to you about Melissa and the flags."

"Melissa and the flags?" Jean repeated, puzzled.

"Yes, and at this point," Lisa said abruptly, "we'll just talk about it at one."

What was that about? Jean wondered after hanging up. *She sounded pretty upset. Did I hurt Melissa's feelings? But what's the big deal?*

JEAN'S UNCOMFORTABLE MEETING WITH THE MANAGERS

Jean was sitting at her desk when Lisa and Kelly arrived for their weekly meeting. Her office was very small because it had a sink and had formerly been used as a nurse's office. The managers pulled their chairs close to Jean's, forming a tight, triangle seating formation. As usual, Lisa started. "We heard that you told Melissa that she has to take down those flags."

"Yeah, I did," Jean responded cautiously.

"Well, that is inappropriate," Lisa stated. "We are not going to tolerate your bringing your political opinions to work."

"I didn't say anything about my political opinions," Jean explained. "I just said I didn't want the flags up."

"That is a political opinion," Lisa asserted.

"I didn't say anything about my political opinions on the war," Jean explained. "I just said I wanted the flags down." *But the flags were never removed anyway,* Jean thought. *When I came in this morning, they were still in the office lobby, but I decided to let it go.*

"Well, you know," Lisa continued, "this brings up a lot of stuff that's been going on with you. I heard from Amanda that you accused Dr. Ash of taking bribes to prescribe Lexapro. And Norma told us that you wanted to change everyone's schedules."

As Lisa continued, Jean began to cry. *What is she talking about?* Jean tried to explain the reason for her concern for the flags, telling about the group discussion the day before and how a political showing might adversely affect clients.

"Oh," Lisa responded, "I didn't realize there was a clinical justification."

Emboldened, Jean continued. "I think that the flag is an important symbol, and I don't want the agency to be showing a political opinion."

"A flag is a flag," Lisa stated.

"Oh, I don't see it that way," Jean responded. "I see the flag as a symbol."

"We're supporting our troops," Lisa said through her teeth. "It doesn't say anything about what we feel about the war. You better not argue about supporting our troops."

"We went to talk to human resources," Lisa continued, "about if we can fire you for bringing your political opinions to work, and they said no."

Kelly had been silent throughout the conversation. And now Jean was stunned silent. The general staff meeting was scheduled to begin in few minutes.

"Take a little time to get yourself together, Jean," Lisa closed the conversation. "We're going to go into this meeting and clarify roles for the staff. We're going to let them know who's in charge."

Jean tearfully pondered whether to walk out of the door or prepare to be humiliated at the staff meeting. *Oh my god!* Her thoughts raced, *They have talked to everyone about me. Boy, are they mad at me. These people don't even understand me. I really don't know what my role is now. How do I salvage my job? Can I assert myself after this?*

9

PRIVATE, DISMISSED

Michelle Hovis and Lori D. Franklin

Social worker Patty Cohen listened carefully as Maria Benavides, the discharge planner, described the plan for veteran Sharease Jackson. Sharease had been hospitalized numerous times since she first came to the Veterans Administration (VA) hospital in 2009, but this time seemed different.

"I just spoke to her about discharge plans," Maria stated, "and, you know, she usually just says she'll be fine, and she's either evasive or hostile about services or engaging in treatment. But this time I mentioned the Mental Health Intensive Case Management Team, which I have mentioned before, but she seemed interested."

Development of this decision case was supported in part by the University of Oklahoma School of Social Work. It was prepared solely to provide material for class discussion and not to suggest either effective or ineffective handling of the situation depicted. Although the case is based on field research regarding an actual situation, names and certain facts may have been disguised to protect confidentiality. The authors thank the anonymous case reporter for cooperation in making this account available for the benefit of social work students and instructors.

"Really?" Patty asked. Patty had previously mentioned this service to Sharease, and Sharease had said, "The last thing I need is more of you all in my business."

"Yeah," Maria continued. "She seemed sad but kind of like she knew she really needed that kind of intensive help and was kind of resigned to it. Maybe she's finally accepted that it's time to start getting better."

"Maybe," Patty said hesitantly. "So what happens with her now?"

"Because she stated she wants to go home and that she does not want to die and has no more plans or thoughts about suicide, she'll go home. We'll set up an appointment with the MHICM Team folks to see her Monday morning."

OVERTON BROOKS VA HOSPITAL

The wars in Iraq and Afghanistan presented a huge challenge to VA hospitals across the country with Operation Enduring Freedom/Operation Iraqi Freedom (OEF/OIF) veterans. New technologies, improved safety equipment, and better battlefield medical care fortunately helped more soldiers survive injuries that would have proven fatal in previous wars. But VA doctors and researchers came to realize that surviving often devastating injuries and prolonged combat deployments caused an unprecedented number of psychological injuries. The government recognized the need for programs to deal with the psychological injuries and created federal mandates requiring all VA facilities to focus on mental health.

Like other facilities, the Overton Brooks VA hospital in Shreveport, Louisiana, had to do major restructuring and program development to deal with OEF/OIF veterans' needs. This VA hospital was relatively small compared to other VA hospitals in the region and had predominately served Desert Storm, Vietnam, Korean, and World War II veterans. But OEF/OIF veterans presented very different needs.

RESPONDING TO VETERANS' EMERGING NEEDS

Across the country, several specialty programs emerged out of the government's recognition of the enormous mental health needs of veterans returning from the Middle East. Although the Overton Brooks VA had staff who could address issues such as post-traumatic stress disorder (PTSD), substance abuse, and other mental health issues, there were no specialty programs or inpatient psychiatric facilities at the hospital. Overton Brooks began developing specialty programs to address not only substance abuse and PTSD, but also the dramatic increase in suicide. In fact, much of the VA and government attention nationwide was focused on suicide prevention. When implementing a twenty-four-hour suicide-prevention hotline, the VA developed the slogan "It takes the strength and courage of a warrior to ask for help" to reduce the stigma of mental health treatment among veterans.

At the same time, the VA system acknowledged the rise of military sexual trauma (MST) and the need to address this issue. The federal government mandated VA hospitals to implement programs and processes that addressed MST. The Overton Brooks VA's answer to the mandate was to hire a registered nurse (RN) as the MST coordinator and require all veterans, male and female, to be screened for MST during primary-care visits. The RN provided education to VA staff and veterans about MST and held a weekly group for victims of MST.

Another major change at the Overton Brooks hospital was the creation of an inpatient psychiatric unit. It fell under the umbrella of the Behavioral Medicine Programs. Behavioral Medicine was charged with managing all the new mental health specialty programs as well as inpatient and outpatient mental health services. All mental health staff—psychiatrists, psychiatric nurses, techs, and social workers—answered directly to the Behavioral Medicine chief, who was a psychiatrist.

The VA system hired more social workers than any other agency nationally, and individuals with an MSW were in high demand. This was true of Overton Brooks VA, which had social workers employed in each of the Behavioral Medicine Programs as well as in primary care, inpatient medical care, and the emergency room. Because of the large number of social workers in each area of the hospital, administrators decided to create a Social Work Department headed by a social work chief. A licensed clinical social worker, the social work chief was charged with managing all social workers in the hospital.

PATTY COHEN

Patty Cohen had been raised in New England, but her family had moved often because of her father's work. The family had eventually settled in Louisiana. Patty's father was a PhD engineer and had high expectations for her. She always knew she would become a doctor. However, life took a different path for her, and she had decided on a bachelor's in psychology and then a master's in social work. Even though Patty worked in the social work field, she always felt a strong pull toward medicine. A few years into her MSW career, she decided to take a shot at medical school and began taking premed classes.

Not long after starting pre-requisites for medical school, Patty was diagnosed with lupus. The physical challenges of her illness and the demands of school proved too much, so she put her medical school dreams on hold and returned to the social work field.

During the nineteen years since earning the MSW, she had worked in many different fields of practice, including medical social work, hospice, home-based mental health, inpatient psych, and corrections (in one of Louisiana's toughest maximum security prisons). She held clinical licensure in both Louisiana and Texas.

Patty was one of the social workers hired during the restructuring of the VA's Behavioral Medicine Programs. She was hired to help open the inpatient psychiatric unit and answered to the psychiatrist, Dr. David Poindexter, who was the Behavioral Medicine chief. Soon, though, after the new inpatient unit was established, Patty was moved to the outpatient mental health clinic. The staff of the mental health clinic included Patty as the only social worker, a full- and a part-time psychiatrist, a physician's assistant, and the part-time MST nurse. The full-time psychiatrist, Dr. Jaul Halim, chaired the outpatient treatment team meetings and was the leader of the clinic. The other psychiatrist, Dr. Carol Dollarhide, split her time between the inpatient and outpatient units. However, because Patty was a social worker, her supervisor was Scott Corey, a licensed social worker and the newly appointed social work chief.

Patty had just sat down at her desk in the outpatient unit when she was paged by the emergency room staff. She walked there quickly, hearing a commotion as she neared the first exam room.

"Get the hell out of here!" Patty heard a voice yelling. As she entered the room, she saw Dr. Chen, a young male resident, standing near a young African American female. Patty guessed that the woman was about five feet three inches tall, weighed about 140 pounds, and had an athletic build. The woman was swinging her IV pole like a weapon.

"Get out of my room, asshole! Don't you dare touch me!" the patient yelled, her eyes looking wildly around the room. She swung and jabbed at Dr. Chen with the pole.

"I am supposed to examine you," Dr. Chen explained. But he began to back toward the doorway. Patty slipped into the room and stood to the side, just inside the door. By now, two security guards had arrived. Entering the room, one grabbed the pole from Sharease, and the other held her arms tightly against her.

"I will not be coming back," Dr. Chen told Patty and turned to walk away.

"Hi?" Patty asked gently, keeping her distance. "He's gone. Are you okay?"

The security guard still held on to Sharease, but she slowly stopped resisting.

"Who are you?" Sharease asked. Her voice quivered slightly.

"I'm Patty, the social worker here. I'd like to talk to you for a while if that's okay." Sharease nodded.

"I think we're okay now," Patty said to the security guards. "I'll call you if I need anything." The guard holding Sharease hesitated but then relaxed his grip and let her go.

"We're fine," Patty repeated, looking directly at the guards. The two men walked out of the room, and Sharease sat down on the bed.

"I'd like to get to know you a bit," Patty began. "I wonder if you need a second, though, first." She sat down quietly in a chair that faced the bed, noticing that Sharease still appeared shaken and nervous. She waited quietly, thinking that might be the best way to intervene.

"Maybe you can tell me first a little bit about what things you like to do?" Patty offered when Sharease seemed calmer. "We don't have to start off with a bunch of questions," Patty said kindly.

"I love reading," Sharease shared. "I'll read anything I can get my hands on, even if it's a dictionary or an encyclopedia. And I love self-help books or anything like that. I like to write, too. I've even had a contract to publish some of my poetry. I just never got around to it."

"I'm a big reader, too," Patty responded. "I have a couple of books in my office that you might like. Maybe when you leave the hospital, you can come take a look."

Patty was soon able to move into more of her typical psychosocial assessment questions and gather information about Sharease's childhood. *I can ask her later more about what was happening when I walked in*, Patty thought. *I want to build rapport first.*

"I was raised by my great-grandma," Sharease shared. "My mom and dad were around some, but both of them were addicts. Mom's kinda cleaned up by now, though, and she lives close by to me. But mostly things were pretty okay. I just always wanted to grow up and join the military."

Patty continued with questions about Sharease's military service.

"I was pretty good at school, so I got out early when I was sixteen. I got permission to join the army at seventeen, just like I had always wanted."

Patty waited for more details, but Sharease got quiet and looked down. "Then by the time I was nineteen, I was discharged. I guess all that was just a dream, and that isn't going to happen for me."

OUTPATIENT THERAPY

Patty agreed to continue seeing Sharease on an outpatient basis in the mental health clinic after Sharease was discharged from the inpatient unit. Sharease attended appointments sporadically, but Patty still felt she was getting to know her.

"I've always just kinda been who I am, and people always knew I was, you know, more into women than men," Sharease stated one afternoon. "Never had been that big of a thing, but some of the guys there in the army would hassle me about it, make crude jokes and stuff."

"Sounds like it might have been kind a big deal," Patty responded, "getting hassled about who you are."

"Well, you know, I just ignored it. They'd call me all those names and whisper behind my back. Sometimes they'd say stuff about how I just needed a man and all that. I just ignored it."

Patty was quiet, listening, suspecting Sharease had more to say.

"Then that one night, they came into my room when I was sleeping."

After a long silence, Patty asked, "Who came into your room?"

"I don't know. There were so many of them, I could never count them. And it just went on and on, one after the other, and I just kinda tried to get away in my head." Sharease's eyes teared up, and her jaw tightened. She looked into the distance.

"It hurt so much, and I tried to fight back, but then I just gave up. I don't even know how long they were there, but it was a long, long time. I just remember waking up, hurting and blood everywhere, and seeing that the sun was up."

Patty was quiet, listening and letting Sharease lead the disclosure.

"Then I went and told my superior officer, you know, thinking he'd help me and all. But he didn't do nothing! Nothing! He just let them keep on saying filthy things to me and didn't do a thing about it. It just got worse and worse. I didn't feel like I had anything left to do but die. There's nothing here left for me."

All the pieces now fit for Patty. After the brutal assault, Sharease's suicide attempts had begun, and she eventually was discharged because of her instability.

THREE MONTHS LATER

Patty had told Sharease about the MST services, but Sharease refused additional appointments. The MST nurse, Kathy Fairfield, worked on Wednesdays doing a group session and a few individual sessions. Although Patty had tried several times to introduce Sharease and Kathy, hoping it would encourage Sharease to talk to her, the connection didn't seem to happen. They met one time for a few minutes, and Sharease had said afterward, "I don't want to meet with her. Just you, Patty. I don't need any more appointments." Patty didn't push her.

Sharease's reputation had built after four more hospitalizations during the three months since Patty first met her. Emergency room staff and hospital staff often said they were scared of her. During one hospitalization, Sharease had become agitated in the emergency room lobby, and when a male staff member approached to try to detain her, she had squirmed away and taken off running through the hospital. She was eventually tackled and forcefully brought back to the intake area. On another occasion, she became angry in the lobby of the hospital and took a flagpole out of a holder on the wall and banged it on the hospital walls, prompting staff in other parts of the hospital to think they heard gunshots in the hospital. She was now required to be escorted by security at all times when she was on the hospital campus.

Once on the inpatient unit, Sharease would quickly be discharged, sometimes within hours of being brought to the unit. If released to the outpatient clinic, she would usually not attend her follow-up appointment.

"I don't want to see Sharease anymore," Dr. Carol Dollarhide, the outpatient psychiatrist, had told Patty. "She's been hospitalized so many times that I know she isn't taking her meds, and she's completely noncompliant. But Dr. Halim told me I can't fire her. I told him that was bullshit because she threatened to kill me. I don't know why I have to keep working with someone who threatened me."

Patty was silent but remembered the conversation with the so-called threat that Dr. Dollarhide referred to. Feeling that having the constant security presence was making things worse, Patty had asked if she could escort Sharease to her appointment with the doctor, with the hope that she would be able to deescalate her if needed. The security guard was still there, but he waited in the hall while Patty went inside the office with Sharease. She remembered Sharease telling Dr. Dollarhide, "Get the fuck out of my face," but Patty didn't consider that a threat. That was just Sharease being herself.

"Well," Patty responded. "I'm happy to keep attending her appointments with her if you think it helps. I've seen her only sporadically with all the hospitalizations, but she does call me pretty often. I think she's taking her meds, but she is still suicidal."

"She is aggressive and dangerous," Dr. Dollarhide responded. "We can't help her here."

"I don't agree," Patty responded. "She's traumatized and vulnerable, and her aggression comes from a place of self-protection. I'm frustrated because I can't work with the trauma when she's so unstable that I can never see her for sessions. She calls me and says things to indicate she is suicidal, and then I have to have her detained. We are just in that cycle."

"Has anything worked with her therapeutically?" the doctor asked.

"Not really. She doesn't want to do any type of evidence-based therapy for trauma, she won't do homework assignments, and I guess I'm not really doing therapy the way I normally do. But she stays in touch with me, she tells me when she is suicidal, and I get the sense that some day she might be ready to work harder in treatment. It is just tough to build trust with her."

"She needs to be referred out, Patty," the doctor responded, sounding irritated. "Maybe to some kind of long-term care facility or something, I don't know. But what we have here is risky and not working."

"I agree that a long-term inpatient trauma program would be great," Patty exclaimed. "Unfortunately, Sharease is not service connected, so she's very limited in the services she qualifies for, and that's not one of them."

"Well," Dr. Dollarhide questioned, "why isn't she service connected if she's claiming all this trauma happened while she was active duty? Maybe we should concentrate on that first."

"She's tried to get a service connection," Patty explained. "She's just never made it through the interview with Disabled American Vets. I think that when she's asked to relive the rape in front of a big panel of men, she panics and runs out of the interview. She would probably qualify, but without that evaluation she's not going to get the service connection. I think for now the only option is to keep seeing her in outpatient and trying to get her to respond to treatment."

BACK IN THE HOSPITAL

Within a few days of Patty's conversation with Dr. Dollarhide and after another missed appointment, Sharease was back in the hospital, this time for another hanging attempt. She had spoken to Patty on the phone and told Patty she felt a lot of uncontrolled anger and sadness. Patty had become concerned enough that she had called Sharease's mother and asked her to go check on Sharease. Her mother had walked in and found her hanging in the closet but got her down before serious damage was done and brought her to the hospital. The intake staff informed Patty that the veteran had been readmitted.

Patty went to visit Sharease and took a book of poems that she thought Sharease might like to borrow. Sharease was sleeping when Patty arrived, so she just set the book on the table. Sharease had a room by herself because she was the only female on the unit.

After leaving Sharease's room, Patty stopped by the office of Dr. Carson, the inpatient psychiatrist treating Sharease during this stay.

Patty knocked softly and asked, "Dr. Carson? I wanted to talk to you about Sharease, if I could."

"Sure, Patty," Dr. Carson said. "We did a Risperdal Consta injection last night to hopefully help her be a little more compliant on her medications. She was pretty agitated last night, so we had to do some tranquilizers, and she should sleep a while."

"OK," Patty said, "I'm just becoming concerned about how quickly she is discharged. As you know, this is her fifth hospitalization in as many months, and it just seems like she isn't here long enough to stabilize."

"I know," Dr. Carson responded, "but if she doesn't meet criteria, we have to let her go. It really isn't our fault that she isn't stable. She doesn't take her meds, and she isn't doing anything to help herself. We're doing the best we can, but you can't fix someone who doesn't want to get better."

"I guess we will staff her case in our outpatient treatment team again if she is coming back soon," Patty responded. "Thanks, Dr. Carson."

TREATMENT TEAM MEETS

The outpatient staff met weekly for a treatment team meeting. As the outpatient psychiatrist in the mental health clinic, Dr. Halim led the meeting, but staff members of other outpatient programs, including a psychologist and a substance abuse counselor, were also part of the team.

"As you know, Sharease has been hospitalized multiple times now," Patty began when her turn came at the treatment team meeting. "For now, she's still there, but they will discharge her very soon, and I think we need a plan for her. We all know that the hospitalizations haven't been going so well. . . . It seems like as soon as . . . "

"You got that right!" psychologist Megan Anderson interrupted. "She's completely out of control. You need to get Adult Protective Services involved here and get her some kind of a guardian and in a residential facility of some sort. I don't know, maybe her mom could step up or something, but she can't be on her own. She's not competent."

"I agree, Megan," Dr. Dollarhide chimed in. "She's dangerous, and I will not see her again. I'm not going to be responsible for an antisocial patient who is so volatile. I'm not going to put the rest of the staff at risk again. We have security with her, and she's still agitated and violent. Nothing has gotten any better."

"But, come on," Patty implored, "she needs help. She's been so severely traumatized. We all know enough about PTSD to know that's affecting her behavior and that it takes some people a long time before they're ready to really do therapeutic work about trauma. I agree that she's not progressing in terms of controlling behavior and reducing her suicidality, but I do feel that I have been developing a good rapport with her. And if it were just a personality disorder, she wouldn't be complaining of hearing command voices telling her to hurt herself, so I just don't think that's all there is to it. I think we should stick with her. I am just not ready to give up on a nineteen-year-old veteran!"

"No one has even talked about substance abuse," substance abuse counselor Marilyn McLain interjected. "I mean, all this behavior could just be from being an addict. I think we need to admit her to some kind of a substance abuse treatment center and get all that stabilized before we can even start thinking about her mental health concerns. It's all too blurry right now."

"I don't think substance abuse is the issue," Patty responded. "She has major trauma stuff going on, and the substance abuse is just a way to cope with that. And I don't even think she does anything besides smoke marijuana and drink on occasion. I agree that it makes her riskier, but it isn't the core problem. She needs to stay in the hospital longer or at least until we think she's safe to release."

"I read Dr. Carson's notes," Dr. Halim stated matter-of-factly, "and no one can see any grounds to keep her any longer. She appears stable today and doesn't meet hospitalization criteria. She's denying auditory hallucinations or suicidal ideation or intent. The injectable medication ought to help her stabilize, but, Patty, you better think of a different plan with her."

VISIT TO THE HOSPITAL

Patty tapped on the frame of the open door and entered Sharease's room. Sharease was dressed in her street clothes and looked at Patty without smiling.

"I hear you're heading home tomorrow," Patty began.

"Yeah," Sharease responded flatly.

"I hope you'll make an appointment with me and come in soon," Patty said. "I know you're tired of the hospitalizations, and I'd like to figure out a plan to keep you doing okay without the hospital."

"I don't know," Sharease stated. "I'm tired of all this. I talk to you, and I just end up here again, so I don't know what good that's doing me."

I don't know either, Patty thought. But she said aloud, "I think it's doing some good. You've made some progress in how you get along with your mom and realizing your role in how that relationship works."

"I guess," Sharease looked at the floor.

"Well," Patty continued, "and I really appreciate that you keep in touch with me and let me know what's happening with you. But let's meet tomorrow at three in my office and decide what we want to accomplish together."

Patty stayed a while and spoke with Sharease, informing her that she would be calling her mother and asking her to check on Sharease daily to make sure that Sharease had her discharge medications and that she knew she was welcome to see Patty when needed.

The next day, a Wednesday, Sharease did not attend her follow-up appointment. Patty left a message on her cell phone but did not receive a return phone call.

On Thursday morning, Patty arrived at work promptly at 8:00. She checked her email and fixed a cup of coffee before seeing her first veteran at 8:30. The veteran, Matthew Vicar, was recently home from combat and was coming in today with his wife to discuss marital issues that had arisen since his return. Patty had scheduled them a little extra time because this was the first chance she had to meet Matthew's wife.

Her session had just started with Matthew and his wife when the phone rang. Patty ignored it, letting it go to voice mail, because she didn't want to be interrupted during a session. It rang again, this time with the double ring indicating it was from within the agency instead of from an outside caller.

"Well, excuse me a second," Patty apologized. She picked up the phone, irritated.

"Patty," operator Latisha said, "Sharease has been calling over and over again. She says it's an emergency, and she has to see you. I have her on the other line."

"Tell her I can see her at 12:15," Patty said, looking at her planner.

"She says she can't wait," Latisha responded, "she's coming right now."

"Well, she'll have to just wait outside until 10:30," Patty said. *So much for that 10:30 meeting*, Patty thought, *but I do want to check on her.*

At 10:30 sharp, the security guard walked Sharease down to Patty's office. Patty was immediately struck by how different Sharease appeared. She was quiet, looking down, not resisting the security guard or even seeming to notice him. She was wearing oversize clothes and looked weary.

"Come on in," Patty said. "It's good to see you."

"I just came by to tell you good-bye," Sharease began abruptly. Patty felt her pulse quicken.

"What do you mean, Sharease?" she asked.

"It's like I'm already dead," Sharease said without emotion. "Like every piece of me except my physical body is dead already, and now I'm just waiting."

"Sharease," Patty asked directly, "are you saying you're going to kill yourself?"

"No . . . ," Sharease's voice trailed off as she looked around the room. "I don't think so, I just think it will happen. Death is inevitable. We all die. Sooner or later."

"Sharease," Patty pressed, "you know that when you say things like this, I can't just pretend I don't hear you. I have to make sure you're safe." Patty knew that Sharease knew the drill. *But this time feels different*, Patty thought. *No emotion, no yelling and screaming about not wanting to go to the hospital, different altogether.*

"Patty, will you write my memoirs?" Sharease asked.

Patty was silent. She thought carefully about how to respond.

"Well," Patty said, "I need to think about that. I don't like to make promises that I can't keep." *Sharease is obviously trying to tell me she's serious. This is not her usual presentation; something's very different.*

Patty assessed Sharease fully, finding that she did indeed present enough of a risk of suicide to require inpatient treatment again. She arranged for Sharease to go to the inpatient unit, and Sharease didn't object at all.

DISCHARGED AGAIN

The next morning Patty called the inpatient unit to see how the intake and first night had gone for Sharease. She spoke to the discharge planner, Maria Benavides.

"She seems to be doing pretty well," Maria said. "She was cooperative, ate a good dinner, and went to sleep. She took her medications and seemed quiet and pretty calm."

"Has she said anything about thinking she's already dead," Patty asked, "or that she's going to die, that sort of thing?"

"No, quite the opposite actually," Maria replied. "I just spoke to her about discharge plans, and, you know, she usually just says she will be fine and is either evasive or hostile about services or engaging in treatment. But this time, I mentioned the MHICM Team, which I have mentioned before, but she seemed interested."

"Really?" Patty asked. Patty had previously mentioned the MHICM Team to Sharease, and Sharease had said, "The last thing I need is more of you all in my business."

"Yeah," Maria continued, "she seemed sad, but kind of like she knew she really needed that kind of intensive help and was kind of resigned to it. Maybe she's finally accepted that it's time to start getting better."

"Maybe," Patty said hesitantly. "So what happens with her now?"

"Since she stated she wants to go home and that she does not want to die and has no more plans or thoughts about suicide, she'll go home. We'll set up an appointment with MHICM to see her Monday morning."

This doesn't feel good to me, Patty thought. *This doesn't sound at all like Sharease. But I don't know what to do!*

IO

WANDERING

Lori D. Franklin and Danielle R. Snyder

"You know," case manager Cheyenne Rowtag began, "this started out as a very simple case. Dionna just needed to take these simple safety precautions. But she's not doing it. She's been on my caseload since November of 2007! We're over a year down the road now, and she can't seem to get her living situation stable. How long are we going to keep these kids in custody?"

Supervisor Richard Maxwell, a licensed clinical social worker (LCSW), looked down at his desk, thinking carefully about what Cheyenne had just said. As her direct supervisor, he knew he had to help her make a decision and that the responsibility for this case was actually his.

Development of this decision case was supported in part by the University of Oklahoma School of Social Work. It was prepared solely to provide material for class discussion and not to suggest either effective or ineffective handling of the situation depicted. Although the case is based on field research regarding an actual situation, names and certain facts may have been disguised to protect confidentiality. The authors thank the anonymous case reporter for cooperation in making this account available for the benefit of social work students and instructors.

"You're right," he replied. "This should have been a simple case. But now here we are with two kids in the home and two out. And we've gone over the gamut from 'send them home now' to 'terminate her rights.' When do we just give up on our treatment plan and say, 'Forget it'?"

LIVING IN NATIVE AMERICA

Gallup, New Mexico, was often called the "Indian Capital of the World" because of the Native American cultures found in and around the town. More than 30 percent of the twenty thousand or so residents were American Indian. Gallup was a common tourist stop for travelers interested in southwestern Native American culture, and it was positioned right on famed US Route 66. The University of New Mexico had a campus in Gallup, and there were other regional colleges in the area.

THE COUNTY AND THE NATION

The Children, Youth, and Families Department (CYFD) of McKinley County provided a wide range of child welfare services, including investigation of abuse or neglect, foster care, permanency planning, emergency shelter placements, ongoing treatment for parents and children, as well as adoptive services. As workers in a community with a large Native American population, the CYFD staff was very familiar with the Indian Child Welfare Act. When a Native American child was brought into custody after a complaint of abuse or neglect, the worker typically would immediately call Navajo Nation Child Welfare (NNCW). The two agencies enjoyed a good working relationship, and the child would usually have a caseworker at both NNCW and CYFD.

NNCW had a central office in Window Rock, Arizona, and five national division offices, three of them located in New Mexico, that helped implement the NNCW's mission. NNCW's goal was to permanently place Native American children in homes that were culturally competent and supportive, allowing children remain connected to their culture.

However, the Navajo Nation didn't have the resources to take full responsibility for all of the Native American children in custody. If the CYFD became involved with a Native American family, NNCW would be notified, and collaboration would begin. NNCW might take responsibility for the case altogether, or it might continue to collaborate with CYFD.

A COMPLEX SYSTEM

The Indian Child Welfare Act required that when any Indian child was removed from a home, the first choice for placement was within a relative's home, and the second choice was another family of the child's tribe. If neither of these options were available, the child could be placed with a family from a different tribe as a third choice. Regardless of whether the NNCW or CYFD had the ultimate responsibility for the case, NNCW also had to approve a placement even if CYFD had certified it according to state and county standards. Because the Native American population of Gallup was large, placement according to these options was less of a challenge than in other parts of the state. But CYFD would occasionally encounter situations where distant kin did not want the child or a Native American placement would disrupt. If a child were moved to a noncompliant home in an emergency, CYFD knew that it would sooner or later have to move the child again when a Native American family became available.

When CYFD remained the primary providers for a family, the case could be heard in a tribal court if a parent requested it. The tribal caseworkers at NNCW usually had smaller case loads and therefore could work more closely with each case, and some parents preferred to work with the tribal court system. The tribal judge made the final decision about whether the Navajo Nation would take responsibility for a case or just continue to coordinate services with CYFD to ensure the child was placed in accordance with the Indian Child Welfare Act.

The workers from both agencies frequently collaborated, and even when a case remained CYFD's responsibility, the NNCW worker would still be informed of progress and be a part of the treatment team. The NNCW worker and the tribal judge remained important figures, especially because all placements and any reunification plans still had to be approved by them as well.

RICHARD MAXWELL, LCSW

As the supervisor of permanency planning, Richard Maxwell was responsible for overseeing the staff who worked all aspects of a case once a child was in CTFD's protective custody. He had been a caseworker at CYFD while he completed his BSW at New Mexico Highlands University in 1998 and then completed his MSW as an advanced-standing student. Now, more than ten years later, he was on the advisory board at the University of New Mexico, a supervisor at CYFD, and a prominent member of the community. Richard was in his fifties; he had gone to school later in life and had quickly transitioned into management. Although he was white, he felt comfortable working with Native American clients, supervisees, and community members. New Mexico Highlands University had an emphasis on social work with Native American peoples, and so that population was part of his educational experience as well as his practice experience. Before his promotion, he was the tribal liaison for the agency and had the responsibility of negotiating the relationship between the two agencies.

CHEYENNE ROWTAG, BSW

Cheyenne Rowtag was a Native American woman, in her late fifties, who had been born and raised in Gallup. She had been classmates with Richard in the BSW program but had never wanted an MSW, stating, "I have enough headaches having to pay for that BSW!" She liked casework and especially liked working with young mothers. Doing her job in a small town with her own community of Native Americans, negotiating dual relationships was a common occurrence for Cheyenne. She came from a large family; her mom had five children by the age of twenty-one, and Cheyenne was the oldest. Cheyenne now had several grown children and grandchildren in Gallup. Before assigning a case to her, Richard would often ask, "Okay, is this one related to you?" Like all the staff, Cheyenne would avoid work with any relatives, but it was unrealistic to expect her never to work with someone she knew.

WANDERING TODDLERS

"Cheyenne," Richard said, walking to her desk among the cubicles outside his office. "I want you to take over this case that just came in from investigations. Looks like these two kids were picked up the other night by the police."

Cheyenne rose and followed Richard back to his office to hear more. She sat where she could see his computer as he scrolled through the investigation report on the screen.

"We have this mom, Dionna, who is Navajo, age twenty-two," Richard began. "Looks like the hotline got a call Tuesday night that the police had picked up her two boys, ages two and three. She's also got a baby in the home. The boys were picked up over on South Puerco Drive in their pajamas about 7:00 PM. They were just wandering around all by themselves."

Cheyenne read along over Richard's shoulder. "If that's her address, looks like they were over a quarter mile away from home. They could have crossed Aztec, which is a busy street, and gone through that ravine over there."

"Yeah," Richard continued, "looks like the police knocked on some doors and couldn't figure out where the kids lived, so they called us."

"So we got the call at 8:30 PM," Richard continued. "Mom says she noticed the kids were gone at about 7:00 but looked around for them until 8:00 before she called the police. So it looks like the police already had them for an hour when the mom called, but they called us instead of taking them home."

"Is the police report in there?" Cheyenne asked.

"Let's see," Richard scrolled down. "Here, yeah, it says 'two children were found outside in their pajamas with no shoes on and with no adults around. Knocked on several doors with no luck finding a parent. One child was in desperate need of a diaper change.'"

"Hmmm," Richard chuckled, "no wonder the police called us right away. They were probably like, 'Come get these kids because we don't want to change this diaper!'"

"What did the mom say happened?" Cheyenne asked.

"Uh, let's see," Richard kept scrolling. "Mom says she fell asleep watching a movie. Okay, so they took the boys, Kevin and Deshon, out to a foster home in Cibola County for an emergency placement. They are two and three, part African American and part Navajo," Richard continued. "Then the investigator went out the next morning, saw there were no locks on the door . . . wait a minute."

"What?" Cheyenne asked.

"It says the investigator found no reason to remove the baby. That's pretty unusual, not to take all the kids if there's an unsafe home. But it looks like they didn't find cause to remove the baby. Well, I guess she just figured if the concern was the kids getting out the door, the baby wasn't mobile yet, so the risk wasn't there. I don't know, though, she's falling asleep early in the evening with three kids there? I don't know, an unusual case here with two kids out of the home and one still in."

"What did the investigator put on the initial plan?" Cheyenne asked.

"Not much," Richard replied. "Get locks on the doors, complete the parenting class, maintain a steady income and housing. Pretty simple stuff."

"Well," Cheyenne said, "ought to be a pretty simple case, and we'll have those kids home soon. We will just have to keep our eyes open to see if there should be any more investigation about the baby being home. But if no risk was found last night, I guess that's where we're at. I will go call Navajo Nation and make sure they're in the loop."

HELPING DIONNA

"So, Cheyenne, can you give me an update on Dionna's case?" Richard asked. "I know last week when we discussed her, you were working on getting her evaluated for depression."

"I scheduled her a doctor's appointment," Cheyenne began. "But when it was time to go, she said she had changed her mind. Then I got a call from her TANF worker saying that since she hadn't completed the workshops, they were shutting off her TANF. So I tried to call her and couldn't get her, so I drove out to her mom's house. She was there, saying she's living there again with the little one and the newest baby. I guess it is good that she's living with her mom after having that new baby, but this makes the sixth place she's lived since we got this case. I asked her about Mitch, Kevin's daddy, and she said he is back in jail and is going to get three years this time. And she says she doesn't know Brian's location, and when I asked her about trying to get child support from him about these two little ones, she didn't want to."

"So," Richard asked, "we're still in the same place with her treatment plan then? Sure doesn't sound like good progress on steady income or steady housing. How do you think she's getting by now? How's she supporting the kids she has?"

"Well," Cheyenne responded, "I don't know how she's getting diapers for those babies. Unless her mother is helping her out. She moves in with friends, then her cousin, and back and forth."

"She goes to court in two weeks, right?" Richard asked, glancing at his calendar.

"Yeah," Cheyenne responded. "I'll be writing up that active attempts have failed and mom has made no progress. I hate that because I'd like to get those kids back home with her, but she just isn't doing anything to show she's stabilized enough."

"Frustrating," Richard said. "It sounds like you have tried to do a lot with her. What about that parenting class she was going to do with the Nation?"

"They wanted to send a parenting instructor to work with her in the home. That hasn't happened yet, probably because she keeps moving around, and Linda from the Nation says that Dionna doesn't return her calls to set up a time."

"Okay. What about the boys? How are they doing?"

"Well," Cheyenne began, "if you recall, they were first with that family out in Cibola County, you know, where the foster home was shut down because of inappropriate discipline?"

"Right," Richard said, "and then they were with the lady out in Manuelito?"

"Yeah," Cheyenne replied. "But she was just temporary while we kept looking for a kinship placement. Mitch has an aunt and uncle who said they'd keep the kids. What is frustrating, though, is that we placed them there, really clearly telling them that we wanted them to be a permanent placement for these kids if it didn't work out with Dionna, but now they are saying they're tired of having them there."

"Tired of them?" Richard asked. "We thought that was going to be a good placement. Good practice, getting those kids with relatives. And now that they've been there a couple months, I sure don't want to move them again. How frustrating!"

"Well," Cheyenne continued, "they assumed the children were going home soon with the mom or dad, and they were hoping it would be the dad. But now that he's going back to prison, I guess they are changing their minds. So now they're all mad, saying I'm not helping Dionna when she's not helping herself. They're trying to blame me when it's really Dionna who's just not making progress. I know they're frustrated that this is taking so long, but I'm really trying hard!"

"I know you are, Cheyenne." Richard responded. He knew Cheyenne had been spending lots of time and energy with this case, but it looked as if it wasn't going anywhere.

"I've transported her to see the kids; in fact, I think all the visits she's had with them have been ones where I drove her out there. I took the child when he had to have that surgery on his teeth and went and got Dionna so she could be there with him. I even offered that one time to take the kids to Dionna's aunt's house so they could visit, and she was like, 'No, I don't really feel like it.' I've given them transportation all the time. I can't believe they are saying I'm not helping."

"I know," Richard said again. "How do we make someone get stable?" He reflected aloud, "It's like she's caught in the system, in a trap, of thinking she can just visit her kids, and that is okay or something. Cheyenne, maybe you should talk to her about the serious consequences of this upcoming court date?"

"I'll try," Cheyenne responded.

TWO MONTHS LATER

"What is Dionna doing to make progress?" Richard asked as Cheyenne sat in front of him, staffing the case. "I mean, I know we helped her pay some rent, but she didn't stay in the place."

"Right," Cheyenne responded.

"And she still has never followed through with TANF?" Richard asked.

"No, she hasn't reapplied since she got kicked off the last time. I'm not sure what to do anymore, Richard. I mean, I have tried to do what I can to support her, and that didn't work. Then I went to court to report on progress, and I was going to say that she hadn't made any, but NNCW didn't support that, saying we hadn't done what we need to do."

"Right," Richard responded. "Then you wrote that letter to NNCW explaining all the efforts we have made, and they went back on that issue about the other kids being there. It's such a mess. I mean, it's a good and valid point, that if the older two weren't safe, why would the little ones be okay? But each of those babies has been investigated and determined as safe. I get why the NNCW won't support termination on the older ones if we are leaving the younger ones in a situation with a parent who was determined as unfit, but then they sure aren't able to do any better than we can about helping get this stuff done for reunification. She just can't seem to do those simple things to get those older ones back."

"So what this boils down to," Richard summarized, "is that we have an original case of poor supervision with some little Houdinis who got out of the house, and we've asked her just to do some basic stuff to create a stable, safe home and have an income, and she can't accomplish any of those things. Yet we still find the home safe enough for her other two kids."

"Yes," Cheyenne replied. "What makes it complicated is that she hasn't taken the steps to do what we've asked to get her kids back, and they're not hard things to do. Most people would have done the simple things we asked them to do to get their kids back, and she hasn't. I don't know why she won't just do it."

Well, Richard thought, *I'm not sure where to go with this. Should we just say, "Forget the treatment plan and take your kids back?" We've asked to terminate before, but are we really going to push forth with termination and placement outside of kinship over a failure to complete the simplest treatment plan? Especially when we really don't think the home is particularly unsafe? But is this mom really going to take care of them if she doesn't want them bad enough to follow through with simple stuff? What is the best thing for these little boys?*

II

A MATTER OF LIFE AND DEATH?

Susy Villegas, Karen A. Gray, and Mónica M. Alzate

Three weeks after Kelly Brown's promotion to unit supervisor at the Kansas Department of Social and Rehabilitation Services, she and Melissa Manning, a child welfare worker, were sitting in Kelly's office staffing a case when Martha Roberts, a child welfare program consultant for the department, unexpectedly knocked loudly and interrupted them.

"I need to talk to you guys," Martha said gruffly, standing with her arms crossed. "What are you going to do with Donna Carlsband's baby?"

"We just finished a home visit, and we're going to set up services," Kelly responded, surprised and perplexed by Martha's sudden appearance and demeanor.

"That baby is going to die if you leave her there!" Martha fumed.

Development of this decision case was supported in part by at the University of Oklahoma School of Social Work. It was prepared solely to provide material for class discussion and not to suggest either effective or ineffective handling of the situation depicted. Although the case is based on field research regarding an actual situation, names and certain facts may have been disguised to protect confidentiality. The authors thank the case reporter for cooperation in making this account available for the benefit of social work students and practitioners.

DEPARTMENT OF SOCIAL AND REHABILITATION SERVICES

The Kansas Department of Social and Rehabilitation Services (SRS) was created in 1973 to replace the Department of Social Welfare and to oversee social services and state institutions. To become part of this new umbrella agency, all offices statewide were consolidated into six regional offices and thirty-five district offices. By 2010, in addition to children and family services, SRS operated adult services, family services, and financial, health, and medical services. The programs that these divisions oversaw included food stamps, child support, Head Start, substance abuse, low-income energy assistance, disability determination, and immigrant and refugee assistance. Child Protective Services (CPS), housed in the Children and Family Services office, was tasked with investigating abuse and neglect cases, and providing services as necessary.

CPS was implementing a new model of practice. This model, which was evidence based, was meant to ensure more consistent services by child welfare staff in the assessment and treatment of families. The model could lead to improved outcomes by providing child welfare workers the skills to be more efficient when assessing families. The new model's main focus was family preservation. Instead of a focus on removing children from their homes to protect them, workers were asked to focus on preserving families and increasing the safety within the homes. Of course, children were still to be removed if the situation were truly unsafe, but the new model emphasized the importance of family attachment much more than previous models for working with families at risk.

To promote the new model, the agency required training for all its workers. Many workers grumbled about the new model because they were being told to respond and react differently than they had in the past. In essence, they were required to develop a new culture in the way they delivered services.

KELLY BROWN, NEW SUPERVISOR

Kelly Brown worked in the Topeka office, and her scope of work fell under CPS within the Integrative Service Delivery System. Kelly embraced the new model of practice being implemented across the state.

She knew it was a time of a huge transition, especially for employees with five to ten years of experience who were accustomed to focusing on the protection of children with less regard for family preservation. Kelly firmly believed that family preservation should be the goal and that the agency's mission was not to raise children. But she also believed that if children were in an unsafe home, they should be placed in a safe home or shelter. She not only agreed with the new model, but felt comfortable using it and was happy about the continuous updates on the new protocols and the training on how to implement them. She was so optimistic about the model's use and implementation in her new unit that she hung a poster of it on her wall, referring to it as needed.

Before coming to SRS, Kelly was a member of a multidisciplinary team at LifeHouse, a nonprofit agency in Topeka that investigated incest, child deaths, sexual abuse, and other high-profile cases. Being on call and visiting homicide crime scenes was intense, but she absolutely loved what she did. Kelly had started working for SRS because she believed she could positively affect more lives there. In the past five years, she had held several positions at SRS, including permanency planner, foster care worker, and child protection investigator. Most were promotions, and she hoped one day to run the agency.

Unlike most SRS workers, Kelly was just twenty-seven years old when she was promoted to supervisor after only her fifth year at the agency. She was also in her final year of the University of Kansas MSW program. She was white and looked her age but had a tranquil manner. Kelly worked long hours and didn't get to see as much of her husband and her dog as she would have liked, but she loved her job and felt passionate about social work.

As soon as Kelly accepted the promotion and was assigned a unit, she began receiving phone calls from friends in other units.

"Kelly," one said, "I can't believe you are taking over that unit. Everyone has grievances filed against all the former supervisors. Those workers are a difficult bunch to work with, AND their work is shoddy. Good luck—you're going to need it!"

Such comments made Kelly pause but only slightly dampened her enthusiasm for the new work. *Maybe they are poor performers and hard to get along with, but I need to find that out for myself. I'm keeping an open mind and a positive attitude.*

In her newest position, she was responsible for the unit's completion of assessments and investigations of child abuse and neglect. Her unit workers included seven employees: two case aides, a temporary employee (who did supervised visitation, transportation, and filing—she was basically a case aide but was paid more), and five full-time child welfare workers. In this new position, Kelly reported to Ralph Green, the senior child welfare supervisor, an African American man with six years of post-MSW experience and fifteen years of child welfare experience at SRS. Kelly's training for the new job involved a three-week curriculum on coaching and management skills, which she completed just before her promotion. She was nervous but confident. With enthusiasm over her promotion and the ideas from her recent supervisory and social work training echoing in her head, she knew it was up to her to train her workers and let them know her expectations.

MELISSA MANNING, CHILD WELFARE WORKER

Melissa Manning was a white child welfare worker in her late fifties with a bachelor's degree in juvenile justice. A single parent of two children, she enjoyed spending time outdoors. Despite her twenty years of experience at the agency, some of her peers perceived her as a mediocre worker, unwilling to put in the time and effort required to do her work well. Kelly knew about these rumors and was not surprised when Ralph, her new supervisor, informed her that Melissa was "office based"—in other words, that she was not allowed to work from home as some employees did because she needed more structure and supervision. Kelly's first encounter with Melissa happened during Kelly's first day at the office. Kelly was moving into her new office when Melissa came by.

Kelly looked up from the box she was unpacking and stepped forward to greet her. "Hello," she said, offering her hand, "I'm Kelly Brown. You must be Melissa Manning?"

"Yes, I just wanted to stop by and say hi," Melissa announced, "because I work from home."

On my first day, Kelly thought, *I'm going to have a battle with this worker*. But she paused and replied calmly, "Actually, I was told that you work from the office."

"No," Melissa retorted, "I don't know why they told you that because I'm home based."

"Well," Kelly insisted, "my boss told me you work from the office."

"Then I can take this up with him," Melissa declared.

"Okay," Kelly responded, "that sounds fine." Though feeling awkward, Kelly consciously let go of the tension.

MARTHA ROBERTS, CHILD WELFARE PROGRAM CONSULTANT

Martha Roberts was a white woman in her midfifties and an experienced agency employee. One of her former positions at the agency was as a family preservation worker, and ten years earlier she had been the worker for Donna Carlsband's cousin, Leela. Now she was a child welfare program consultant, a "sounding board" whose responsibility was to staff cases, yet without formal supervisory authority over unit supervisors or frontline workers. Because she traveled to many office sites, she dressed sensibly. "No need for heels and suits or flashy jewelry in this line of work," she told colleagues.

Martha had a reputation for yelling at people and for being hot-tempered. During her years at the agency, she had seen firsthand how things could go wrong in a case, despite the agency staff's best intentions. She was particularly sensitive about deaths of children while in state care and the ensuing media scrutiny of the agency's actions. She and Kelly had interacted in coalitions before Martha became a program consultant, but they had never worked together much. Kelly had always staffed cases with another agency worker, whom she viewed as her mentor, instead of using expert consultants such as Martha that SRS had assigned. Kelly's mentor, Debbie Cottor, was Martha's former boss.

THE CARLSBAND FAMILY

From Donna Carlsband's old file, Kelly learned that Donna's early childhood was chaotic and that she had been in and out of foster care because of sexual abuse by her father. Following the investigation,

Donna's father was forced out of the home. As Donna grew older, she lived with her mother and her cousin Leela, who had moved in with Donna's mother and father a few years earlier. Much older than Donna, Leela was developmentally delayed and had children of her own. Leela's parental rights were terminated because of allegations that she, teenaged Donna, and Leela's boyfriends were having sexual interactions in front of Leela's children. Later, while still in her teens, Donna had begun having children of her own. Over the course of nine years, her four children were removed at varying times due to neglect. For example, she fed the children soda pop instead of formula, which led to failure to thrive. She also often left her children with unsuitable caregivers. Donna tried to complete her service plans, but Donna's boyfriends were another worry to the agency. As an adult, Donna had a history of relating with men who put her children at risk. She would meet a man on the street, and within a week he would be living in the home with her children. There were also concerns that Donna was working as a prostitute. Her parental rights were eventually terminated for all four children, and the case was closed.

THE REFERRAL

On Tuesday, an intake worker received a hotline call regarding the Carlsband family from Donna's cousin, Leela. She reportedly told the worker, "My cousin just had a new baby with her new husband, Steve. They've been married two years and live in their own apartment now. But when Donna was pregnant, they lived with me and her mom and dad. When they were here, Steve got pissed off one night and said, 'I can't stay here anymore! I'm leaving!' then he opened the closet door real fast and hard to get his clothes and hit Donna in the face with his elbow, breaking her nose, because she was standing behind him. So I called the police, and Steve was arrested. I'm just worried about that new baby."

Kelly received the new report from the intake worker and the old files on Thursday and assigned the case to Melissa. Melissa read the new report and the old files for Donna and Leela and staffed the case with Kelly.

Although there were no allegations of injuries or neglect to the baby, Melissa thought that the age of the baby and Donna's parenting with four other children warranted an investigation and a home visit. Kelly agreed and instructed Melissa to set an appointment when both of them could go.

The next day Kelly received a call from Gloria Fox, a supervisor with whom Kelly had previously worked at another office. Gloria had supervised Donna Carlsband's case ten years earlier. When Gloria had heard about Donna's new baby, she was very concerned. Furthermore, when she'd heard that Melissa was the worker, she doubted that Melissa would take the case seriously enough, so she decided to call Kelly.

"I think you need to look back over the case history," Gloria cautioned. "I am very concerned that your unit may have a child death on your hands if you're not careful."

"We're looking into it and are about to visit the family," Kelly assured her.

"You really should remove the child," Gloria insisted. "I know that family, and that child is at great risk! You don't want to be reading your name in tomorrow's paper, do you?"

At that point, Kelly became more concerned and decided to staff the case with Ralph Green, the senior child welfare supervisor. He agreed with the plan to conduct a home visit to check on the child's safety.

"I think this is a good idea," Ralph said, "and you could also see for yourself how Melissa interacts with the family."

"That's what I was thinking, too," Kelly responded. "But just because a parent has a termination does not mean that it's an automatic removal."

"Exactly," Ralph concurred, "every situation is a case-by-case basis."

THE HOME VISIT

Following up on the concerns, Kelly and Melissa traveled together to the Carlsband home and met Donna, Steve, and their son. The first floor had just a couch, a loveseat, a coffee table, and a kitchen table. Baby formula was stacked on the kitchen table. The baby had a little blanket and car seat. In the upstairs bedroom, there were only mattresses. The walls were bare. Donna was of average build, five feet three inches tall, a white woman with long stringy hair to the middle of her back. After Steve had shown them the house, Kelly noticed that Donna was sitting on the couch, holding the baby and hunched over. *She looks like a mouse in the corner afraid to make a move,* Kelly thought, *as if someone's going to jump out and snatch the baby.*

Melissa interviewed Donna and Steve while Kelly observed. Donna said she was feeding the baby formula, had maintained her Women, Infants, and Children appointments, and had obtained the resources the hospital suggested, such as clothing and child care equipment. She confirmed the domestic abuse incident that was documented in the case file.

"I pled guilty to assault or domestic violence," Steve explained, "because my lawyer told me that it was easier and cheaper to plead guilty than go through the process of a trial. I went to a program at the YWCA, and I can show you the letter saying I finished the program."

"This does not seem to be a matter of life and death," Melissa told Kelly on the ride back to the office. "Plus, they signed up for parenting classes before we even got this referral."

"We should give the family every opportunity to succeed," Kelly agreed. "We need to make sure Donna has a chance. This means a comprehensive support plan that includes a family preservation worker who would make home visits every week."

NEXT STEPS

Back in Kelly's office, as Kelly and Melissa were completing their assessment, Martha knocked loudly on the office door and interrupted them.

"I need to talk to you guys," Martha said gruffly, standing with arms crossed. "What are you going to do with Donna Carlsband's baby?"

"We just finished a home visit, and we're going to set up services," Kelly responded, somewhat surprised and perplexed by Martha's sudden appearance and demeanor.

"That baby is going to die if you leave her there!" Martha fumed. "Kelly, don't be such a Pollyanna! This woman has proven again and again that she can't care for her children, and just because she's older and married to some abusive man doesn't mean she can parent. I mean, my God, she used to have sex with her cousin and a parade of 'boyfriends'—many of whom were tricks—in front of her babies! Any one of those men could have been a child molester or worse. Those children thrived in foster care and now are in great adoptive homes. You don't want to be the next Linda Gillen[1] do you?!"

---

1. Linda Gillen was an SRS worker who was sued by the family of a child who died in state custody. See T. Potter, Coffeyville couple sues SRS worker after granddaughter's beating death, *Wichita Eagle*, January 24, 2010, http://www.kansas.com/2010/01/24/1150653/coffeyville-couple-sues-srs-worker.html#storylink=cpy, retrieved January 28, 2012.

12

EXPOSED

David Pooler and Terry A. Wolfer

The day had been very stressful. It was nearly time to go home, but psychiatric social worker Steve Giodorno still had to do something that had been on his mind all day.

He needed to talk with the parents of his patient, seventeen-year-old Alex Landham, about what they wanted for their son. Dreading the phone call, he stepped outside the hospital and felt the hot August sun shining on his face. Hands in his pockets, he mentally rehearsed what he needed to talk about with them. He took a deep breath, ran his fingers through his hair, and slowly walked back inside. The butterflies were intense.

Development of this decision case was supported in part by the University of South Carolina College of Social Work. It was prepared solely to provide material for class discussion and not to suggest either effective or ineffective handling of the situation depicted. Although the case is based on field research regarding an actual situation, names and certain facts may have been disguised to protect confidentiality. The authors thank the case reporter for cooperation in making this account available for the benefit of social work students and practitioners.

After he dialed the Landhams' number, the phone rang only once.
"Hello?" It was Cindy Landham, Alex's mother.

"Umm," Steve began, "this is Steve Giodorno. I need to discuss what happens next with Alex."

Cindy's silence seemed deafening.

BIRMINGHAM, ALABAMA

Birmingham stood in the heart of the Deep South. Founded in 1871 at the crossing of two railroad lines, the city blossomed through the early 1900s as it rapidly became the South's foremost industrial center. With abundant natural resources, Birmingham was a natural fit for iron and steel production. As an industrial town, it had suffered greatly in the Depression, but after World War II the city had experienced moderate growth. The workers at the area's legendary iron and steel mills were increasingly replaced by a workforce of medical and engineering professionals. The new Birmingham enjoyed a balance of manufacturing and service-oriented jobs in a thriving economy. Through all the economic ups and downs, though, it retained its strong southern character. In 2000, it was the largest city in Alabama, with a population of 232,820 and a metro area population of more than one million.

CARRAWAY METHODIST MEDICAL CENTER

Carraway Methodist Medical Center was a large hospital that served the Birmingham metro area. It offered comprehensive medical services, including the Bradford/Carraway Behavioral Health Units, which incorporated an adolescent inpatient psychiatric unit with twenty-two beds. Most of the admissions came from downstairs in the emergency room, but occasionally there were direct admissions from some local psychiatrists or community mental health centers. The average stay for patients was seven to ten days, but some patients stayed as long as thirty days.

This locked unit was staffed with nurses, mental health technicians, mental health counselors, teachers, social workers, and a psychiatrist. The staffing configuration varied based on how many adolescents were placed on the unit. Depending on the unit census, there were up to three nurses. The registered nurses (RNs) and licensed practical nurses did the intakes on the new admissions and monitored and distributed medications. Likewise, depending on unit census, there were up to two mental health techs and three mental health counselors. The mental health techs generally took vital signs, and the mental health counselors monitored patients' whereabouts on the units and completed general family assessments on those newly admitted. So that patients could continue their schooling, two teachers taught morning classes Monday through Friday.

The staff also included two psychiatric social workers, Steve Giodorno and Vicki Knable. They worked with hospitalized patients on the inpatient psychiatric unit who suffered from mental illness or substance abuse problems or both. Their daily tasks were to complete psychosocial assessments in which they spoke with both the patient and, if possible, his or her family. In addition, they were responsible for discharge planning, starting from the time of admission, to ensure an appropriate referral upon treatment completion. On the unit, the social workers led daily individual and group therapies. If they obtained information about physical or sexual abuse or neglect, as mandated reporters they were required to report it to the Department of Health and Human Services, the local child welfare agency.

Finally, the staff included several psychiatrists who made decisions on the pharmacological regimen for patients and oversaw their treatment plans. The unit manager, Bobbie Coggins, RN, supervised everyone on her unit but the psychiatrists.

STEVE GIODORNO

Steve Giodorno finished his MSW in May 2000 at the University of Alabama, with coursework concentration in direct practice and adolescence. Steve had gone straight through bachelor's and master's programs and was a good student. After completing his MSW internship at Bradford/Carraway, he thought, *This place will work for me and fits me well.* He accepted the job offer Bobbie presented to him as he finished his MSW. Because Steve completed his internship there, he had already encountered many different challenges on the unit and felt confident in his abilities. Steve was thorough with patients and invested in their well-being and treatment. Sometimes he would stay hours after his shift ended to ensure that patients received excellent care.

After fifteen months, Steve still loved working at Carraway. With straight brown hair and a muscular build, he looked snappy and professional. Now twenty-four years old, he was bright and energetic and wanted to make sure that Bobbie Coggins was happy that she hired him.

TUESDAY MORNING, MEETING ALEX LANDHAM

After saying good morning to Trish, the nurse on duty, Steve briefly met with Vicki to decide who would get which cases from overnight admissions.

"I think this one is for you," Vicki said and slid the paperwork for Alex Landham across the counter. Steve looked at the handwritten note on top of the chart, which said, "white male perp., suicidal ideation." An unwritten policy was that, when possible, Steve would work with the boys who were violent or had sexual issues, and Vicki with girls who had sexual issues. Steve had dealt with suicidal ideation numerous times, but the "perp" note left him feeling more anxious than usual. Because of reported inappropriate sexual behavior, Steve knew the adolescent unit staff automatically considered Alex a perpetrator. As a result, he was not allowed to have a roommate on the unit. Furthermore, unit staff would place him on a close observation checklist for sexual acting out ("COC-SAO" on forms).

To prepare for talking with Alex, Steve opened the chart and read through the notes recorded by the intake nurse. The chart read: "pt. masturbating in front of 9 y/o sister, father caught pt. . . . pt. and father argued about the sexual acting out. . . . pt. tearful, embarrassed, and ashamed. pt. said, 'I don't want to live anymore' and ran off upstairs. pt.'s mother and father transported him to ER at 8:40 pm, pt. cooperative."

After reading through the chart, Steve still felt anxious but intrigued. *What's going on? Is this the only time, or has it happened before? Have other kids been involved? Females? Males? How will this kid respond to an interview?*

As was standard procedure, Steve walked over to the classroom and asked Beth, one of the teachers, if he could take Alex out for further assessment. She pointed him out to Steve. Alex was a tall, sturdy, well-groomed seventeen-year-old. He was wearing a gray, buttoned, short-sleeve shirt and a nice but faded pair of jeans and some brown-colored clogs.

Steve approached Alex and spoke softly to minimize the classroom disruption. "Hey, Alex, I'm Steve Giodorno, one of the social workers, and I need to get some more information from you. We can talk in the office." Adhering strictly to the unit's no touch policy, Steve did not shake hands when introducing himself.

"Sure," Alex responded, "it will be good to talk with you."

In the hallway, Steve added, "I know you've talked with a million people already, but unfortunately I've got to get some information from you as well."

On the way to his office, Steve informed Rick, one of the mental health counselors, "I have Alex, and I'm taking him to my office." The social work offices were located between the adolescent and children's units, outside the locked doors of either unit. As usual, Steve left the door to his office open while they sat down to talk.

"How's it going here?" Steve began. "I know you just got in last night. Are you doing okay?"

"It's all right," Alex responded.

During the psychosocial assessment, Steve asked, "How are you doing in school?"

"I only have six credits after two years of high school because of failing classes," Alex reported. "I'm not doing great."

"Have you been in trouble in school?"

"I've never been in any major trouble, but I've been to detention a few times."

"Have you ever been arrested?"

"No."

"Who lives at home with you?"

"Well, my dad."

"What does he do?"

"He's retired from the military, but now he works at the post office, and my mom stays at home because she can't work."

"Do you have any brothers or sisters?"

"Yeah, I have two older brothers who live on their own."

"Anyone else?"

"Yeah, my nine-year-old sister lives at home."

"So tell me what brought you here," Steve probed further. *This behavior seems so out of place for such a nice kid, and it clearly shocked his family.*

"My parents brought me."

"Why did they need to bring you?"

"I felt suicidal about something that happened last night," Alex replied somewhat haltingly. "My dad found me in my sister's room doing something with my sister."

"What kinds of things were you doing with your sister?" Steve asked.

"Well," Alex hesitated for a moment, "I had my sister pull her pants down."

"Were you clothed?" Steve probed.

Looking away from Steve and toward the floor, Alex acknowledged, "My pants were down."

"And what were you doing?"

"I was masturbating," Alex replied sheepishly.

"Did you have your sister touch you?"

"No. I made her look away from me when I masturbated," Alex paused. "I asked her to pull her pants down and turn her back to me and lean over the bed so I could look at her butt."

"Did you touch her?" Steve asked firmly.

"No," Alex replied.

Steve probed further, "Have you done this before?"

"Yeah, I have," Alex responded slowly.

Curious and concerned, Steve asked, "How did you get your sister to do this for you?"

"One day while she was playing with toys," Alex said, "I just asked her to pull her pants down, and she did it."

What do you get from this, Steve wondered, *masturbating in front of your sister?* Out loud he continued, "So, Alex, tell me about what you were feeling last night. The chart says you were talking about hating yourself and wanting to kill yourself."

"I feel guilty for what I did," Alex explained. "I hate what I did. I'm embarrassed. I love my sister and never wanted to hurt her."

"How did you plan to hurt yourself?"

"I thought about combining chemicals to drink."

"Have you ever had thoughts of hurting yourself before?" Steve asked.

"Yes," Alex explained, "about eight months ago, after my girlfriend broke up with me, I thought about combining Ajax and Clorox to drink."

Steve asked, "What made you think of doing this to yourself?"

Alex replied, "I know the military uses these types of chemicals, so I figured I could use them."

Through the next hour, Steve learned that Alex was a rising junior in high school, was employed at one of the local movie theaters, and had several close friends. He acknowledged having tried pot a couple of times and having used alcohol but said he was not a regular drinker. Even though Alex had dated one girl about two and a half years and, more recently, another girl for three months, he reported that he had not been sexually active with anyone.

As the interview neared its close, Alex asked, "What's gonna happen? How long am I gonna be here?"

Steve gave the standard response, "Well, it's different for everybody, sometimes seven to ten days depending on your issues." Then he added, "We need to see what your parents are feeling about you returning home."

"Mr. Steve, I know I did something wrong, and I'm ready to face whatever it is I have to face. I know I'll never do it again. I'm so glad that I'm finally getting help. Thank you, thank you, Mr. Steve."

Can I be sure he won't do this again? Steve wondered silently. "I think you'll fit in here just fine. Just try to make the best of this experience. I'm very happy to hear that you are accepting responsibility for your actions and not blaming anybody else for what you did. Try to make the most of being here by participating in therapies and learning what you can about yourself. This is also a nice little break from your family . . . sort of a vacation . . . where you can make some changes in your life."

I kinda like this kid, Steve mused after returning Alex to the classroom. *He's a lot like my best friend from high school. He reminds me so much of Todd.*

Knowing he needed to talk with Alex's family, Steve called the number in the chart.

"Hello?" Alex's mother, Cindy, answered the phone.

"Hi," Steve began, "I'm Alex's social worker, Steve Giodorno, and I'm calling to get some more information from you so I can better understand what's going on, so we know how best to treat your child."

"Oh, okay," Cindy replied.

"Tell me about what happened last night," Steve began. "What did you see happen?"

"Jason, my husband, went to get the kids for dinner and found Alex masturbating in Katherine's room," Cindy spilled the story. "Jason started yelling at Alex and told him what he was doing was wrong. I've never seen Jason so angry. It was a little scary, and maybe Jason overdid it with Alex. Jason and Alex were arguing, and I didn't hear everything. Then they came downstairs, and Alex was crying and said he wanted to die. I've never heard my son talk like that before, and we were really worried. I love Alex more than anything, but we are so confused!" After a sob, "Damn it, I'm so mad at him."

"I got acquainted with Alex this morning, but can you tell me about you, your husband, and your daughter?"

"I'm not working because I have diabetes and a congenital heart defect that is mostly controlled by medication, but stress makes it worse. I have to keep my stress low, and this situation is pretty over-whelming. Since we moved here from Yardley, Pennsylvania, seven years ago, I've been hospitalized four times for my heart. I also had a nervous breakdown and was hospitalized twice. My husband is a supervisor at the Bessemer Post Office, and he retired from the army three years ago. My daughter is nine and in third grade, and she's a great kid, and, damn it, I don't believe that this happened." Rais ing her voice, "What the hell was my son thinking?" After a pause, "Now we're putting Katherine in counseling to help her deal with this. I'm sorry. Normally I'm not like this, talking so much. We just don't know what to do with Alex's problem. How can Alex come home after doing this?"

WEDNESDAY

Wednesday evening, after a particularly busy day at work, Steve returned Julie Wallace's call. Julie was a grad school friend who lived in Mobile. They regularly called each other to talk about their lives and work. Julie worked at a treatment center for sexually abused children. After hearing a tantalizing report about a new seafood restaurant in Mobile, Steve told Julie, "I've got a serious case I'm working on," and briefly outlined what was happening.

"You've gotta get him assessed," Julie exclaimed, "by a specialist who works with sex offenders and can complete a Psycho-Sexual Risk Assessment."

"Why would he need that?"

"He's a pervert, doing this in front of his sister! You can't just send him home. You need to find out if he's at risk to reoffend."

"Come on, Julie, he didn't touch her." *You're overreacting,* Steve thought but didn't say. *Since starting work at the treatment center, you think everyone's a pervert.*

"I think you're missing some major warning signs," Julie insisted.

"I don't know," Steve felt his stomach drop. "Alex's behavior seems more bizarre than malicious. You think he's a true offender?" Still doubtful, he wondered privately, *Wouldn't a true offender have touched his sister and maybe even tried to have sex with her, too?*

"Yes," Julie said more quietly now.

"Well, who can do this kind of assessment?"

"There are at least two places in Birmingham that I know of that can do it."

After getting their contact information, Steve said, "Well, thanks, I'll check into it."

After hanging up the phone, Steve worried, *Maybe this is more serious than I thought.*

THURSDAY

The next day, as suggested by his friend and colleague, Steve called and arranged for a Psycho-Sexual Risk Assessment with one of the local practitioners.

After another call to the Landhams, it became clear to Steve that Alex's mother and father felt increasingly angry with Alex. His parents were concerned because Alex was guarded and seemed to avoid talking about his specific behavior in group. And they did not sound all that open to his coming home right now.

For that reason, Steve spent most of the morning trying to find a group home for Alex. Alex was too old for most of the group homes, and when Steve mentioned the sexual acting out, one group home staffer after another indicated that a group home placement was out of the question.

I'm not sure I can do all that much for Alex, Steve began to worry. Just before lunch, Steve called Lilly Fortner, an intake worker at Health and Human Services, to get her opinion on a hypothetical case.

After Steve outlined the case, Lilly responded, "If this is not a situation in which the family failed to protect the daughter, then we would not get involved. You just need to call the police because it's child on child."

The parents obviously didn't know that Alex was masturbating in front of Katherine until the other night, Steve had to agree, *but what good would it do to get the police involved?*

MONDAY

On Monday morning, Steve and Alex had another counseling session. Among other things, Steve decided that it was important that he explore Alex's sexual behavior further.

"We talked earlier about your relationships, and I would like for you to tell me more. So have you had a lot of girlfriends, Alex?"

"A few. Really only two serious ones."

"So have you ever been sexually active with a girl your age?"

"No," Alex replied, "my girlfriends did not want to have sex, and I really didn't try to, so it just never happened. I guess I was trying to be a nice guy. You know, respectful. I would never make a girl do something if she didn't feel she was ready. I want to be in love when I have sex for the first time."

"You said you were dating a girl who broke up with you around the time you began to masturbate in front of your sister. How did you handle the break up?" Steve asked.

"I was really upset and pissed off after my girlfriend broke up with me. She couldn't even give me a reason. I think she liked some other guy."

"Okay, let's talk more about your behavior with Katherine. When you masturbated in front of your sister, did you ejaculate?"

"I've ejaculated only two or three times in my life," Alex replied, "and never in front of my sister."

"Why do you think you were unable to do so?" Steve asked.

"There must be something wrong with me," Alex replied, "I just can't."

"How long have you been masturbating in front of your sister?" Steve asked.

"I'm not sure, about a year."

"So, during this time, you never touched your sister?"

"No."

"How did you keep yourself from touching her? It must have been very difficult?"

"No, I would never touch my sister. I just liked to look at her butt. I never wanted to hurt her or anything. Since I have this problem with ejaculating, it just never was an issue."

"What do you mean?"

"Since I couldn't ejaculate, it didn't seem like what I was doing was that big of a deal."

"But didn't you say you felt guilty about what you were doing?"

"Well, yes, but it wasn't like I was really hurting her."

How can this be true, Steve felt confused, *masturbating in front of your sister for a year and never ejaculating or touching her? Are there medical issues, or is this psychopathology? I just don't buy this.*

ANOTHER CALL TO THE FAMILY

Later that day Steve called the Landhams again to gauge the family's current response and this time to explicitly raise the placement issue. After nearly a week in the hospital, Alex was clearly more stable and no longer expressed suicidal ideation. And that made it necessary to explore Alex's options for discharge.

The phone rang only once. "Hello?" It was Cindy.

"Umm," Steve began, "this is Steve Giodorno. I need to discuss what happens next with Alex."

Cindy's silence seemed deafening. But then she said, "We are not really ready for him to come home yet—I mean, eventually, but not yet. We think he still needs more help."

"As you know," Steve explained, "we are having a difficult time finding other placement options due to his problem. We are unable to find a group home to take him, and he is not appropriate for many other facilities. Could he come home? Or are there some other family members who could take him?"

"We don't have any family near us who could take him, and we don't want him to live in another state."

"There is another side to this issue," Steve offered. "We may also need to call the police."

After a painful silence, she asked, "How can getting the police involved be a good thing? He should be getting help, not sitting in jail! What kind of help would he get there?" After a brief pause, she added, "Dear God, this situation is bad enough; we don't want the police involved."

After concluding the conversation with Cindy, Steve leaned back in his chair. The creaking seemed much louder and more grating than usual. The events of the past week swirled through his head. *I want to do the right thing, whatever that is. What is my obligation, legally and ethically? And what is best for Alex?*

I care about this guy, Steve realized. *What happens if the police get involved? Is he really a sex offender? Should he be arrested? I'm a good therapist. Can't I just handle this without getting anyone else involved?*

"Aww, what should I do?" Steve asked out loud, as he flipped through the Rolodex.

13

NOWHERE TO SKATE

Laura B. Poindexter and Terry A. Wolfer

"I need to go talk to the family now," social worker Kevin Cooke insisted, "but I'll call you back, Kathryn." Walking back to the living room, Kevin took a deep breath and thought to himself, *Okay, here it goes . . .*

When Kevin returned to the living room after talking with the family's Department of Social Service (DSS) caseworker for about five minutes, he found that fifteen-year-old Mitch and his mother had grown quiet. Anne was crying softly, and Mitch simply looked frightened. *They must be worried about what I'll do after talking with Kathryn,* Kevin thought.

Development of this decision case was supported in part by funding from the University of South Carolina College of Social Work. It was prepared solely to provide material for class discussion and not to suggest either effective or ineffective handling of the situation depicted. Although the case is based on field research regarding an actual situation, names and certain facts may have been disguised to protect confidentiality. The authors thank the anonymous case reporter for his cooperation in making this account available for the benefit of social work students and instructors.

As Kevin sat down, he was not quite sure where to begin. That's when he noticed Mitch's shirt was ripped at the left sleeve, exposing his shoulder and a freshly burned cross "tattoo." The burn measured about one inch by one inch, and it was still inflamed and puffy.

FRENCH BROAD COMMUNITY MENTAL HEALTH

In 2000, French Broad Community Mental Health (FBCMH), located in Riverton, North Carolina, was one of twenty-nine public facilities statewide, each of which served four to seven counties. FBCMH had nearly five hundred employees in four divisions: Developmental Disabilities, Child and Family Services, Adult Services, and Substance Abuse Services. Professional employees included primarily clinical social workers, licensed professional counselors (LPCs), and several psychiatrists. The offices of the Child and Family Services Division were housed in a large, relatively new, two-story brick building. Clinical staff did not yet have their own computers; instead, they kept handwritten case notes or typed notes and other reports and documents at shared computer kiosks.

FAMILY-BASED SERVICES

The Child and Family Services Division of FBCMH employed approximately 150 professionals in several units, including a total of sixteen therapists in the Family-Based Services (FBS) unit. Maureen Johnson, a licensed clinical social worker (LCSW) and a fifteen-year employee of the agency, had supervisory authority over all the FBS therapists. FBS was subdivided into a school-based unit (eight positions), a non-grants-funded unit (five positions), and a grants-funded unit (three positions). She was immediate supervisor to the non-grants-funded therapists, and the immediate supervisors in the school-based and grants-funded units also reported to her. Within the grants-funded unit, one therapist worked with domestic violence cases referred by the police department, one worked with families recently reunified by DSS but who were in immediate crisis, and one worked with families of runaway youth. These three positions were funded through specific state grants, and the supervisor of the grants-funded unit oversaw the extensive paperwork necessary to keep the grants going.

Referrals to the school-based unit came directly from the schools, but the other, non-grants-funded FBS therapists provided services to families with children ages zero to seventeen referred by many other sources in the community. With the exception of the grants positions, all of the positions within FBS were Medicaid funded. Families receiving services through the grants were billed if they had Medicaid, but services could be provided to any family through the grants at no charge.

In the FBS unit, about half of the therapists were LCSWs and the rest were LPCs. Everyone in the unit was "family centered" and shared a family-preservation philosophy. They provided most services in clients' homes, and even the school-based staff interacted with the entire family unit as much as possible. Many of the children and youth served by FBS therapists saw FBCMH psychiatrists at the office for medication oversight, as facilitated by the therapists. At least once a month, therapists and psychiatrists would meet together with the family during office visits so that these services were integrated into the overall service delivery.

The entire FBS unit met once a week for staffing cases, and therapists also met individually with their immediate supervisors once a week. Overall, the unit had a strong group of therapists with a broad range of backgrounds and experiences. The FBS therapists generally enjoyed working on this unit, mainly because of the expertise and support shared among the group in staffing meetings and informally in their offices.

THE HAVEN

The Haven Runaway and Homeless Youth Shelter, located only a few blocks from FBCMH in downtown Riverton, was founded in the early 1990s by Grace Episcopal Church. The church had initially supported the program, but after a few years it had turned over its operation to Children's Trust, a nonprofit agency that oversaw several local residential youth homes. For one dollar per year, the church leased the Haven house to Children's Trust.

The Haven served as the only runaway shelter for Riverton and several surrounding counties. It sheltered runaway adolescents ages thirteen to eighteen. It was an old Victorian house that had a family room, dining room, kitchen, activity room, an office, and six beds in three upstairs bedrooms. As a short-term emergency shelter, the Haven kept youth for up to one week. Homeless youth would sometimes stay at the shelter, but most of the adolescents had a local family from which they were running away. The Haven focused on resolving problems so that youth could be reunited with their families. Because the Haven provided only brief crisis-intervention services, its staff made frequent referrals to other agencies and programs in the area, including juvenile justice, DSS, and FBCMH.

The Haven relied especially on the therapist in FBCMH's Family-Based Services unit to provide longer-term follow-up services for youth and their families who seemed appropriate for such intervention and who agreed to participate in the service. Once the Haven referred clients to the FBS therapist, the therapist negotiated continued involvement with youth and their families. If clients agreed to services, the FBS therapist assumed case responsibility when the adolescent left the Haven and returned home. About 15 percent of all the Haven youth and families opted to continue services through FBS.

KEVIN COOKE, MSW

Kevin Cooke thought the grant-funded FBS runaway position was a dream job of sorts. He had been born in western North Carolina and raised in Georgia and Tennessee. Although he had left the Southeast for about eight years, he had recently returned to the area to be closer to his family. Upon returning, he had worked as a foster care worker with DSS for two years before the therapist position opened up with FBCMH. Kevin most enjoyed working with "hard-to-reach" adolescents and had specialized in this population while at DSS. He had known about the FBS position focused on runaway youth since moving to Riverton and immediately applied for it when he saw the ad in the paper.

Kevin had taken an unconventional route into social work. First, he had earned an undergraduate degree in English, with plans to become a teacher. While pursuing a master's degree in English, he had worked for an Upward Bound Program, making home and school visits. In hindsight, Kevin recognized those visits as his first exposure to the field of social work. After graduating, he moved to Washington, DC, to teach English at a community college. While in Washington, he had also volunteered at a lesbian, gay, bisexual, and transgender youth organization and helped staff a hotline for youth in crisis. He later worked as an editor in the publications department at a large non-profit advocacy organization that employed mostly individuals with an MSW. There, he learned more about the social work profession and came to admire the National Association of Social Workers Code of Ethics.

As a result of these experiences, Kevin decided to pursue an MSW. He moved across the country to enroll in a two-year MSW program in advanced generalist practice focused largely on advocacy and community-level work. Upon graduation, he expected to find work as a community youth advocate or organizer. When he returned south to the mountains of North Carolina, only the DSS had job openings. Realizing that DSS could provide a good foundation for his social work career, Kevin decided to accept a foster care caseworker position at Green County DSS just outside Riverton. Somewhat to his surprise, he enjoyed the work and stayed for more than two years.

Now in his early thirties and working toward his LCSW, Kevin came into the FBS runaway grant position with a great deal of enthusiasm. There, he had four to six cases at any one time and typically followed each youth and his or her family for up to six months. He visited families in their homes for one-and-a-half to two-hour sessions two to four times per week. Kevin's intervention would often be the first community service the youth or family had ever received. Kevin worked conjointly with DSS in approximately 20 percent of the cases, and juvenile justice also often became involved with runaway youth and families at some point. He used crisis-intervention methods to help facilitate the youth's return home and then followed with a brief, solution-focused family-preservation model of practice. Any service that Kevin provided was completely voluntary on the part of the youth and family. He often worked with the parent(s) or other caregiver(s) and the child separately at first and then brought them together as a family to work on issues underlying the youth's running behavior. His first task at the Haven usually was to prepare a youth and family for the youth's return home and a longer, home-based involvement with the family.

GETTING ACQUAINTED

The day Kevin began working at FBCMH, LeeAnn Morgan, his immediate supervisor, invited him along for the initial home visit with the Jamison family. It was the early fall, and the mountain leaves were just starting to turn; school was back in session for many FBS clients.

Like Kevin, LeeAnn was just starting a new position within FBS. She had been one of the five non-grants-funded therapists and was now taking over as supervisor of the three grants-funded positions, reporting to FBS supervisor Maureen Johnson. LeeAnn had also been filling in during the runaway job vacancy, handling any referrals from the Haven, and she would continue to see a limited number of FBS families even as a supervisor. Because this was Kevin's first day at work, she intended only to have him observe her interaction with the Jamison family, and she would keep the case. As they neared the Jamison's residence located in Crooked Fork, a beautiful and isolated community about thirty minutes from Riverton, LeeAnn told Kevin what she had learned about the family in their interview at the Haven.

"The Haven called me because Mitch ran away from home," LeeAnn began. "This was actually my first referral from them since the position's been open. Mitch Jamison is a fifteen-year-old who's estranged from his father, Micah."

"What was the cause of the estrangement?" Kevin asked.

"Micah has a drug and alcohol problem and visits his family only sporadically," LeeAnn explained. "He and Mitch's mom have been separated for some time. When Micah does visit, he often fights with Mitch's mom, Anne. Mitch reports sleeping with a knife under his bed because he's afraid that Micah will try to kill him, his mom, and his brother."

Kevin listened intently as LeeAnn continued.

"DSS became involved with the Jamison family after the police came to the home during a fight between Micah and Anne. Reportedly, Mitch had gotten in between Micah and Anne during an argument, and that's when Micah severely choked him."

"Oh my gosh," Kevin responded.

"After the incident," LeeAnn said, "Micah was to meet with a social worker and complete certain tasks for the case to be closed with DSS, but Micah never did anything, so the case is still open. As far as I know, Micah hasn't been around at all since that incident."

"What about Anne?" Kevin inquired. "Does Mitch have a good relationship with his mother?"

"Mitch has a lot of trouble with her, too," LeeAnn reported. "Apparently, they fight constantly, and that's supposedly why he ran away from home."

LeeAnn went on to tell Kevin that Mitch had gotten suspended from school at the very beginning of the school year for incessant back-talking and had been expelled a few days later for refusing to take off his baseball cap when a teacher asked him to do so. He struggled academically and had few school friends. Most of his friends were older and had dropped out of school.

When they arrived at the Jamison's trailer, which was perched on the side of a mountain in a cove off a gravel road, Anne was sitting on the floor in the living room with her face in her hands. Mitch and his brother, eleven-year-old Tom, were screaming and fighting, running in and out of an open sliding glass door leading to a covered wooden deck that served as the main entrance to the home. Kevin immediately noticed that Mitch was small for his age. He had a very striking face, a dyed shock of blondish brown hair, intense blue eyes, and multiple piercings in both ears.

"You're a crybaby!" Mitch yelled at Tom while poking at him as they ran in and out of the house. Actually, Tom seemed to alternate between laughing and crying.

"Mom, make him quit," Tom shouted. "Make him quit!"

"You boys need to settle down and quit that horsing around and come in the house!" Anne interjected. "We have company!"

Turning to LeeAnn and Kevin, Anne said, "I can't deal with this anymore. I want him out of the house." Once they began the interview, the boys quieted a bit but continued to run around.

A very pretty woman in her midthirties, Anne resembled a miniature Shania Twain, both in looks and voice inflection. She had lived in Crooked Fork her whole life and worked as a school aide at Crooked Fork Elementary.

LeeAnn tried to do a formal FBCMH intake with the family, sitting on a tiny clear space on the couch with a notebook and several forms. Kevin sat on the floor because all other spaces were already covered with clothes, books, shoes, basketballs, and skateboards and because Anne was sitting on the floor, too. LeeAnn persisted with the intake process despite the chaos, asking a lot about Mitch's problems and the stress they were causing to the family. Both Kevin and LeeAnn tried to engage Mitch in conversation, but this wasn't possible because he and Tom were so unfocused and running in and out of the room—sometimes playfully, sometimes violently, hitting, slapping, and grabbing at one another. But LeeAnn mostly completed the forms and arranged a follow-up appointment for a few days later.

"I wasn't even going to give you a case right away," LeeAnn said on the way back to the agency. "But since you have this really good background at DSS, and in the intake you were really talking about stuff, and since you like adolescents . . . I wonder, would you like to take this case?"

"Sure," Kevin responded, "it's better than sitting around reading the agency policy manual all week." He and LeeAnn laughed.

WORKING WITH THE JAMISONS

As Kevin began to work with Mitch and his family, he soon realized that Mitch did not fit in physically with other teen males and would get picked on for the way he dressed, his small stature, and the multiple piercings in his ears. Mitch's hair was curly and mostly dark, but he changed it a lot; sometimes he grew it long and then cut it really short, and sometimes he dyed it. Whereas other teenage boys from the community wore tight Wranglers, belts, and even cowboy boots, Mitch preferred baggy clothes and a skater look. Whereas other boys drove pickup trucks, listened to country music, used chewing tobacco, and played sports, Mitch was devoted to skate boarding and heavy thrash-metal music. In a traditional, rural environment, Mitch stood out as an unconventional kid.

Kevin also saw that Mitch and his eleven-year-old brother, Tom, contrasted sharply. Tom had reddish hair and a fair complexion. As Kevin learned over time, their differences went deeper. Tom was academically gifted, had many school friends, and played basketball. He got along well with his mother, whereas Mitch seemed to blame her for his parents' separation. Mitch's friends enjoyed smoking pot and drinking, whereas Tom hung with more conventional peers. Among his group of friends, Mitch was well known for his skateboarding, and he looked down on sports and "jocks." Mitch also differed from Tom because he desired a relationship with their dad, but Tom did not. Mitch easily intimidated Tom because Mitch was strong and wiry, and Tom was soft and slightly overweight and would cry easily.

As the holidays approached, Mitch was still not in school, but things had calmed down some at home. After working with Mitch and Anne for about three months, Kevin believed he had established pretty good relationships with them, and the next step seemed to be to figure out how Mitch could best continue his education.

As best Kevin could tell, he was the first professional to try to interact with this family on a deeper level. He found it easiest to work first with Anne and Mitch separately and then to bring them together to talk about problems in the household. Kevin typically would first meet with Anne when Mitch was outside or in his room listening to music. With Anne, Kevin focused on building her confidence in parenting by setting boundaries with rewards and consequences for both Mitch and Tom. With Mitch, Kevin focused on helping him to express how he felt about himself within the context of his family, peer group, and school setting. He had begun to help Mitch talk more openly with his mom about his feelings regarding both his parents and their breakup.

In their time together, Kevin and Mitch would often take a walk. Sometimes they would go downtown to record stores or to the skateboarding shop, or Kevin would take Mitch and Tom to a park where the boys could skateboard. Mitch enjoyed telling Kevin in great detail about a skateboard feat and then demonstrating it at the park. Tom would skateboard as well, and Mitch would assume a more older brother role than he often did at home. He seemed to feel special having Kevin and his little brother around when other kids were there because he was older than most kids at the park, and he had people with him whom he could show off to. Kevin also had a cool car and could take him and Tom to places the other kids in Crooked Fork couldn't often go.

Kevin liked the challenge of building therapeutic relationships with Mitch and Anne, balancing these relationships so that Anne didn't think Kevin was being "too easy" on Mitch and Mitch didn't think that his mom and Kevin were ganging up on him. Mitch and his mom were getting more comfortable with working on family issues together, and Tom seemed relieved that the daily family upheaval was calming down some.

THE CRISIS

One Thursday, Kevin had a routine home visit scheduled with the Jamisons for 4:00 PM, shortly after Anne arrived home from work. While en route from his office to their trailer, Kevin received a page from the front desk at FBCMH. Kevin returned the call, and the secretary reported that the Jamisons' caseworker from DSS was trying to get in touch with him. Because his cell phone reception was breaking up as he neared the Jamison's, Kevin decided to return the call from the trailer.

When he arrived at the home, Kevin could hear an argument as he walked up to the deck and the sliding glass doors that opened onto the living room. Nevertheless, he knocked and let himself in, as he had grown accustomed to doing when they had a scheduled appointment. In sharp contrast to other recent visits, he did not walk into a peaceful situation. In fact, the commotion reminded Kevin of his first visit to the trailer.

"I can't do this anymore," Anne said forcefully, looking at Kevin. "I don't know what's going on with him."

"She thinks I'm crazy," Mitch screamed.

"You are f'ing crazy!" Anne yelled in return.

"Everybody thinks I'm crazy," Mitch continued. "I'm not crazy. I'm tired of everybody telling me I'm crazy. I just wanted a tattoo!!"

In the midst of their argument, before Kevin had a chance to ask what they were upset about, he heard his pager go off again. It was the family's DSS caseworker calling his pager number directly this time.

When Kevin remarked about this out loud, Anne said, "I know why she's trying to get in touch with you. I told her about what Mitch did yesterday, and she thinks he needs to go to the hospital."

In the background, Mitch continued shouting, "I'm not f'ing crazy! You're a crazy bitch!"

"I think you should talk to her," Anne encouraged.

"Well," Kevin said, "let me call her to see what's going on."

Because Kevin's cell phone wouldn't work in isolated Crooked Fork, he asked to use Anne's phone. She directed him to a phone in her bedroom, which was behind the kitchen at the back of the trailer.

Kevin had met the Jamison's latest DSS caseworker, Kathryn Smith, a few weeks earlier at her office downtown. Probably in her fifties, she seemed competent but rather stern and humorless, he remembered. Though he had only limited experience with Kathryn, Kevin doubted that she related to teenagers very well.

When Kevin returned her call, Kathryn explained that she had called Anne earlier that afternoon about some DSS forms that Anne was supposed to sign. "While we were talking, Kevin, Anne reported that Mitch had burned a 'tattoo' in his arm. This is clearly self-mutilation," Kathryn continued, "and you need to take him to the emergency room and have him admitted to the adolescent psych unit."

"Well, I just got here," Kevin said. "Let me figure out what's going on, and I'll call you back."

"No," Kathryn responded. "The way Anne described things to me, you need to do something immediately. You need to go to the hospital and admit him to the psych unit."

"I need to talk to them and figure out what's going on, and then I can call you back," Kevin repeated.

While he was talking with Kathryn, he noticed that the noise from the living room had completely subsided.

"This is an emergency, Kevin. I don't understand your hesitancy with this," Kathryn said.

Kevin could feel himself becoming angry and a bit defensive as he said, "Kathryn, I know this family pretty well. This family has had three DSS caseworkers in three months, and none of them has invested any time in getting to know the family's situation as I have. In fact, Kathryn, you've met them only once, and I don't think you've been here to the home!"

"Kevin, this isn't a time to bring up whatever issues you have with DSS in this case. You have to act," Kathryn responded. "Now."

Anne overreacts so much of the time when anything happens with Mitch, Kevin thought to himself. *She probably just let out her frustration while on the phone with Kathryn even though things with Mitch really are improving.*

"Kevin? Kevin? Are you there?" Kathryn asked.

"Yes, I'm here," Kevin said, "I just don't want to overreact to this, Kathryn."

Anne was probably more worked up about the situation because of Kathryn's heightened response, Kevin continued thinking. *And Mitch is probably reacting to his mother's reaction.*

"Kevin! My butt is on the line here," Kathryn insisted. "We have a safety contract with this family, so we've got to do something. Besides, you know Mitch's history, so I don't want you to minimize this."

Kevin knew exactly what Kathryn was referring to. Mitch had a history of cutting and burning himself. He still had a scar from an old cut of a rock band's name on his forearm. Kevin thought to himself, *What if Kathryn is right about this, and I've missed something?*

"But Anne, Mitch, and I have talked about Mitch's cutting, Kathryn," Kevin said. "I tried to get him to see a psychiatrist at FBCMH, and neither he nor Anne would agree to it."

"Kevin, maybe you're in a bit over your head here. . . . Are you the only one treating this family? I really think something needs to be done quickly," Kathryn persisted.

Mitch has never been hospitalized for his cutting behavior like other youth that I've worked with, Kevin thought. *I've never had reason to believe that he's suicidal. Besides, I've already discussed this with my colleagues in staffing and supervision more than once. But, still, what if I am in a little bit over my head?*

"I need to go talk to the family now," Kevin insisted, "but I'll call you back, Kathryn." Walking back to the living room, Kevin took a deep breath and thought to himself, *Okay, here it goes . . .*

When Kevin returned to the living room after talking with Kathryn for several minutes, he found that Mitch and his mother had grown quiet. Anne was crying softly, and Mitch simply looked frightened. *They must be worried about what I'll do after talking with Kathryn,* Kevin thought.

As Kevin sat down, he was not quite sure where to begin. That's when he noticed Mitch's shirt was ripped at the left sleeve, exposing his shoulder and a freshly burned cross "tattoo." The burn measured about one inch by one inch, and it was still inflamed and puffy.

14

DRIVEN TO DRINK

Terry A. Wolfer

As a social worker at Jackson County Hospital (Missouri), Lisa Silver had grown accustomed to a certain amount of commotion at work. But this was annoying. Lisa thought she recognized the voice of Carol Davis, a social worker from Jackson County Division of Family Services (DFS), in the registration area. For some reason, she had been talking and laughing, loud enough to be heard above the usual din for at least ten minutes.

As a service to busy DFS workers and police officers, Lisa allowed them to bypass registration and come directly to her office for assistance with abused and neglected children. Finally, Lisa went out

---

This decision case was prepared solely to provide material for class discussion and not to suggest either effective or ineffective handling of the situation depicted. Although the case is based on field research regarding an actual situation, names and certain facts may have been disguised to protect confidentiality. The author thanks the case reporter for cooperation in making this account available for the benefit of social work students and practitioners.

and reminded Carol that she didn't have to stand in line with the other patients.

Carol laughed, "Oh, yeah! I got mixed up!"

That was when Lisa first suspected Carol had been drinking.

JACKSON COUNTY HOSPITAL

Located in downtown Kansas City, Jackson County Hospital was a huge facility sprawling across two city blocks. As a major teaching facility for the University of Missouri at Kansas City and a Doctor of Osteopathy Medical School in Kansas City, the hospital offered numerous stand-alone residency and fellows programs in addition to rotations for medical students. For example, after four years of medical school and earning an MD, a physician might do a three-year residency to develop a specialization in pediatrics. After completing the residency, the physician might specialize even further by completing a fellowship to become a pediatric cardiologist. Both residents and fellows earned salaries for this additional on-the-job training. As a teaching facility, the hospital also provided many services through specialty clinics, including pediatrics. Over the years, several Jackson County Hospital physicians had gained national recognition for their published research on physicians' roles in child abuse investigations. As a public-health facility, the hospital served many indigent clients, who increasingly, because of changing local demographics, were Mexican American.

Lisa's office was located near the main registration desk at Jackson County Hospital, where some four hundred patients checked in each day for their clinic appointments. Children often arrived crying and upset; sometimes staff hollered patients' names. The registration area was always very busy and often noisy, especially in the morning. People waited in line for as long as thirty minutes. It was very often smelly with unwashed patients. Because the registration desk was right inside the main hospital entrance, there was additional traffic unrelated to outpatient registration. Although the walls were painted with colorful murals, they couldn't hide how worn the linoleum was or how old the desks and computers were. The computers inevitably went down once a day.

Since earning an MSW at the University of Missouri at Columbia, Lisa Silver had worked for seven years in the Pediatric Clinic at Jackson County Hospital. As the pediatric social worker, she was also assigned to the Pediatric Emergency Room, a specialized unit designed to provide emergency services for children. About 25 percent of Lisa's social work cases required making routine referrals for resources (e.g., food, diapers) or helping undocumented people deal with the Immigration and Naturalization Service or seek US residency. But 75 percent of her cases involved allegations of child abuse and neglect. For these cases, Lisa was part of a team that evaluated children for abuse. Her role included coordinating hospital services. Lisa typically collaborated with a medical resident: she interviewed the child regarding his or her abuse while the resident completed a medical assessment. Many abused or neglected children were brought to County Hospital by DFS workers for expert assessment, usually by appointment, but sometimes as walk-ins. Other cases of abuse or neglect were found during routine medical care. When DFS or the police were not already involved, Lisa had to ensure that both were appropriately informed of these cases. She sometimes had to advocate on behalf of child patients with either DFS or the police and often made outpatient referrals for follow-up services.

As the social worker in the Pediatric Clinic, Lisa reported to Diane Hughes, supervisor of the hospital's Social Work Department. Lisa in turn supervised Denise Ulmer, the BSW assistant in the clinic.

Some of Lisa's relationships with DFS workers and police were more than professional. They occasionally socialized outside of the hospital after hours. For example, Lisa's best friend for several years was a sex crimes detective who also coached her soccer team. As a result, she saw him several times per week outside of the hospital.

A DISRUPTIVE SOCIAL WORKER

One day in mid-November 1998, soon after 9:00 AM, a commotion in the registration area caught Lisa's attention. Carol Davis, a DFS worker about the same age as Lisa, had transported a three-year-old foster child to the hospital for a walk-in assessment. That in itself was not unusual. But something about Carol's manner was. She was talking very loudly and with more animation than usual; she slurred her speech and laughed a bit too hard at her own jokes. *In fact*, Lisa thought, *she's acting drunk.* And when she called Carol into her office, a more confined space than the registration area, she smelled alcohol on Carol's breath.

Lisa had never before had reason to suspect problems with Carol. Although never close, they had known each other for several years and always got along well. In fact, Lisa believed that Carol did her job adequately, unlike some DFS workers. An African American, she kept her long hair straightened and was consistently well dressed.

While Carol waited for a physician to see the child she had delivered to the hospital, Lisa asked Denise whether she smelled alcohol on Carol's breath. She did. But several nurses said later that they had not noticed alcohol on Carol's breath.

At any rate, Lisa did not confront Carol with her suspicions. Following completion of the medical assessment, Carol drove the child back to the emergency shelter. Almost immediately, Lisa regretted letting her do this. As she remarked to Denise, "It was bad enough that she was driving at all, let alone having a foster kid with her!"

CONFRONTING THE PROBLEM

Unlike the supervisor she had been hired by, Lisa believed that her current supervisor, Diane Hughes, was "not so good." Now with seven years of practice experience, Lisa didn't want help from her very often. In this situation, though, she was not sure what to do. So that afternoon, Lisa went to talk with her supervisor.

Lisa started by saying, "I think I screwed up." Then she described the morning incident and her concerns.

After some discussion, the two women agreed that Lisa should call Carol's supervisor to report her concerns. Lisa promptly tried to reach Carol's supervisor, Randy Burgess, but could only leave a telephone message with his secretary, saying it was urgent that she speak with him today.

When Randy returned Lisa's call the following day, she described the incident in detail. Uncertain about what to do, Randy said that he would consult with his own supervisor, Dale Bailey. Because Randy did not seem surprised by Lisa's report, Lisa wondered whether Carol had done something like this before.

Later that day, after talking with Dale, Randy called Lisa back to suggest that she talk with Carol herself. As Randy explained, "You're the one who observed the problematic behavior, so you really ought to confront Carol about it."

"She's your employee!" Lisa disagreed.

Randy suggested that Lisa, Diane, Randy, and Dale meet to discuss it.

"I'll think about it and get back with you," Lisa said. Now the ball was back in her court. Lisa knew she probably should have said something to Carol the day before, when she first became concerned. But Lisa realized that she hadn't confronted Carol because she didn't know how.

After hanging up the phone, Lisa felt stuck. The more she thought about it, the less she liked how this was going. On the one hand, she was deeply concerned about a DFS worker (or any social worker, for that matter) drinking on the job. In this case, it only further jeopardized the health and well-being of an abused child. On the other hand, talking with the person herself didn't seem to be the appropriate response. Despite what Randy said, this issue still seemed to her to be something the social worker's own agency needed to address —a supervisor's problem. *Besides*, she wondered, *what difference would talking with Carol make, anyway? If she was drunk, she isn't likely to admit it. So then what?* At the same time, Lisa knew that other things smelled like alcohol (e.g., certain medications, mouthwash). Lisa thought, *I'm pretty sure that Carol was drunk, but what if I'm wrong?* Lisa was used to making tough decisions—daily—but this one stumped her. And she really did not want to deal with it.

As the day wore on, Lisa grew angrier about the whole situation. While driving home that afternoon, she fumed aloud, "I'm pissed that I've been put in this position—pissed at Carol, Randy, Dale! It's not my job to be supervising DFS workers! This job is stressful and crazy enough as it is. How could a social worker screw up like this?" Finally, she felt angry with herself for endangering a child's life. "I messed up. Screw Carol."

Although Lisa felt angry with Carol, she also knew about secondary trauma and understood how it could undermine a professional's performance. She had experienced it herself. Especially during the first few years at Jackson County Hospital, it seemed that she had cried over a case either at work or at home at least once a week. She dealt with the horrors she saw at work—babies starving to death, children beaten so badly they had one big bruise from the back of their knees to their waist, babies with third degree burns from being dunked in a hot bathtub as potty training, children tortured by automobile cigarette lighters, a five-year-old doubled over in pain saying, "I'm such a bad boy" (he was in the hospital six months for internal injuries), a fourteen-year-old girl sexually abused by every male in her extended family—more and more by forgetting about the child. She obviously couldn't forget them all. But sometimes only a week after interviewing a child with a resident, the resident would ask if she'd heard anything more about the child, and Lisa would respond, "I don't know who you're talking about." She had neither the time nor the energy to follow up on patients they saw, anywhere from six to twelve children per day.

The next day Lisa went to talk with Diane again. As Lisa suspected, Diane confirmed that it was not Lisa's job to confront Carol now. It was now an issue for Carol's superiors. Having worked at DFS for several years herself, Diane knew Randy Burgess and Dale Bailey personally, so she called them. The supervisors, both of whom were white males, reportedly told Diane they were afraid Carol might "pull the race card" if they confronted her about drinking on the job. When Dale asked whether he and Randy could meet with Diane and Lisa at the hospital, Diane agreed.

At this meeting the following day, Diane and Lisa basically reiterated that it was Randy and Dale's responsibility to deal with Carol. They encouraged the two men to consult their policy people. But it seemed apparent that Randy and Dale had no intentions of following through.

What should I do? Lisa felt responsible but wasn't sure that she was. She had tried to bring the problem to DFS's attention. *But they aren't going to do anything about it!*

15

"DON'T TELL HER"

Sean Siberio and Terry A. Wolfer

Hospice social worker Robin Jean Williams headed to the UniHealth Ventilator Unit on Friday around 11:00 AM. She felt drained at the end of the long week of classes, work, and internship, and she was not looking forward to today. Earlier in the week Robin had been assigned Mrs. Haye, a terminally ill amyotrophic lateral sclerosis (ALS) patient whose husband, Bernie, her health care power of attorney, had decided that she should be taken off the ventilator. Bernie, however, did not want his wife to be informed of his decision, an issue that had created a divisive debate among the hospice team.

Development of this decision case was supported in part by at the University of South Carolina College of Social Work. It was prepared solely to provide material for class discussion and not to suggest either effective or ineffective handling of the situation depicted. Although the case is based on field research regarding an actual situation, names and certain facts may have been disguised to protect confidentiality. The authors thank the case reporter for cooperation in making this account available for the benefit of social work students and instructors.

When Robin arrived, she met with Becky, the hospice case manager, who told her that Bernie wasn't there yet, despite assuring them he would be there at 9:00 AM. Buddy Porter, Mrs. Haye's son from a previous marriage, was already in the room, along with his wife and their two children, ages five and six. It was apparent that Buddy had been crying as he sat at the foot of the bed.

Speaking softly, Robin introduced herself to Buddy and his wife and briefly explained her role. "I'm here," Robin explained, "to assist with any issues you have as far as burial arrangements or resources for those grieving. I'll try to support you during this difficult process the best I can."

"Thank you," Buddy said.

As they stood at Mrs. Haye's bedside talking, Mrs. Porter blurted out, "I believe she should be told what's going to happen . . . because what about her soul?"

You're kidding me, Robin thought. *So the family's divided about this, too?*

"What do you think?" Robin asked Buddy.

Without answering Robin's question, he posed his own. "What would you do?"

"I really can't tell you what to do," Robin paused. "Bernie doesn't want her told. But maybe there's a way for you to talk to her without going against your stepdad's wishes."

"I'm on the power of attorney, too." Buddy responded.

She gave you power of attorney? Robin wondered silently. *Is this really happening? Now what?! I don't want to create more confusion!*

UHS-PRUITT

UHS-Pruitt was a Southeast regional leader in long-term health care. Since opening its first nursing home facility in 1972, the company had grown to include more than seventy postacute, skilled-nursing, and assisted-living residential facilities as well as an array of supplementary services, including home health care, end-of-life care, rehabilitation, veteran care, and consultative pharmaceutical services. The facilities and services were scattered across Georgia, Alabama, and the Florida panhandle.

UHS-Pruitt administrators understood that patients' needs change over time. To help patients and their families manage these changes, they developed a continuum of services enabling patients to receive uninterrupted care, from their own homes to end-of-life, wherever that might be. Over nearly four decades, the company had also weathered numerous changes in the economy, politics, and health care policy and had adopted continuous medical innovation to maintain best-care practices.

AUGUSTA HOSPICE

Augusta Hospice was part of UHS-Pruitt. It provided hospice services to terminally ill patients residing in their own homes, in long-term health care facilities (both Pruitt and unrelated facilities), or in hospitals. Its funding came from private insurance, Medicaid, Medicare, and private donations. Augusta Hospice had offices in both Augusta and Waynesboro, Georgia.

The Augusta office was fairly small, serving on average thirty clients split between two nurse case managers. Besides the two full-time registered nurse (RN) case managers, the staff included a director of nursing, two nursing assistants, a chaplain, and a social worker. Augusta Hospice offered comprehensive services to its clients, including pain management and managed nursing care within nursing homes. The social worker and chaplain provided spiritual support, grief counseling, financial counseling and assistance, as well as family counseling to patients and their families.

PAM WESSINGER

Pam Wessinger, a forty-four-year-old white woman, was the social work administrator for Augusta Hospice but was based at the Waynesboro office. In sixteen years with Pruitt, Pam had performed many roles for the company, including regional director of hospice services for Georgia, Alabama, and Florida. But she had little experience in direct client care, performing mostly managerial and administrative functions. No longer committed to the travel required of a regional director, she had stepped down to be social work administrator for the Waynesboro and Augusta hospice offices. Although based at the Waynesboro office, she made twice-monthly visits to the Augusta office.

NATASHA DINKINS

Natasha Dinkins, a thirty-year-old African American woman, was the unit's director of nursing. After earning an RN from the Georgia Health Sciences University, she had worked in several medical settings. She had joined Augusta Hospice in early 2007 and was promoted to her current position as director of nursing in November 2009. Natasha often stated that she wished to "change the culture" around the unit but never said exactly what that meant. As a new administrator, she was "all business," but still pleasant and outgoing.

Some staff members thought Natasha viewed death differently from other hospice employees. One time in informal conversation, she had admitted not wanting to attend her own grandmother's funeral. She reportedly had attended only after her father insisted that she be there.

BECKY HUTCHINS

Becky Hutchins, a thirty-five-year-old white woman, was one of the two RN case managers. Though she had worked at another hospice for several years, Becky was new to Augusta Hospice. In fact, she was still within the ninety-day probation period. Other staff already recognized Becky as easy-going, funny, irreverent, and rather unconventional. Short and wiry, she often wore revealing outfits at work and repeatedly dyed her hair, often in bold primary colors. She talked openly about some tough family problems: she had reportedly lost custody of her two school-age children because of partying and other behavior. The family problems distracted Becky when she was at work and caused frequent absences, which led to tension with Natasha and disciplinary intervention.

Robin Jean Williams, a thirty-one-year-old white woman, was the hospice social worker at the Augusta unit. Robin had an associate's degree in liberal arts from Low Country Technical College (2000), a BSW from Columbia College (2004), and a master's degree in health administration from the University of Phoenix (2007). A licensed BSW social worker, she began attending the University of Georgia's two-year MSW program after deciding that the health administration degree was not what she needed to advance her career. She was twice divorced and had an eight-year-old son, Mark.

Robin had worked for Augusta Hospice for nearly three years, beginning one year before she started the MSW program. Working at the Waynesboro office, she found the volume of cases to be manageable and relatively straightforward. Once she started the MSW program, she continued at the Waynesboro office as an employee and fulfilled her student intern hours there. The university permitted an employment-based internship on the condition that it involved new and completely separate tasks, so Robin took on the role of volunteer coordinator for her internship. When she transferred to the Augusta office for her second internship, she found not only a higher volume of cases, but increasingly difficult ones with complicated ethical, medical, and legal issues.

UNIHEALTH POST-ACUTE CARE OF
NORTH AUGUSTA

UniHealth Post-Acute Care of Augusta was another Pruitt facility. UniHealth had a total of 126 skilled nursing beds in the facility, including 28 in a ventilator unit. The ventilator unit was one of only four in Georgia, and it received a wide variety of referrals from nursing homes, hospitals, and other facilities in Georgia and South Carolina. The building was more than forty years old, but Pruitt had initiated major renovations soon after buying it in 2008. The ventilator unit, however, was brand new, having been reopened only a few months earlier.

THE HAYES

Allie Brigs, the caseworker at UniHealth Post-Acute Care of Augusta, had called Natasha to inform her of a client who might be in need of hospice services. Allie explained that Mrs. Haye, a fifty-one-year-old white woman from Wrens, Georgia, had resided in UniHealth's ventilator unit for two years, and her husband, who held the health care power of attorney, had recently made the decision to turn off the ventilator. Mrs. Haye was originally diagnosed with ALS at age forty-four. Over time, her condition had slowly worsened. When establishing a living will, she had explicitly chosen not be put on a ventilator. But at age forty-nine, she was hospitalized on an emergency basis, no one could find the living will, and so doctors put her on a ventilator for stabilization until the legal issues could be resolved. Mrs. Haye had been on the ventilator for two years at the time that hospice services were contacted. Despite being on the ventilator, she could still communicate with her husband and nursing home staff members via a variety of means, including use of the assistive boards for ALS patients, blinking, and simple nods of the head.

Mrs. Haye's husband, Bernie, was also from Wrens. When Robin met him, he was wearing a buttoned-up flannel shirt and beat-up jeans. In talking with staff at the nursing home, Robin learned that the Hayes had never divorced, but Mrs. Haye had eloped with another man and subsequently wiped out the Hayes' joint bank account. Soon after eloping, she was diagnosed with ALS and then returned to her husband and asked if he would provide her care. Bernie reportedly told UniHealth staff, "I take care of her out of obligation. There's no love between us." Nevertheless, Mrs. Haye gave him health care power of attorney. Although Mrs. Haye had had no children with Bernie, she did have a son, Buddy Porter, from a previous marriage. He was in his midthirties, and she had seldom seen him in recent years.

In November 2009, UniHealth encouraged Bernie to arrange hospice care for Mrs. Haye, but he declined, believing that she still had hope. By January 2010, however, her condition had deteriorated significantly, resulting in complete paralysis, skin breakdown, and open wounds. She had lost ability to communicate with staff and now required a feeding tube to get proper nutrition.

"After meeting with us a second time, Bernie agreed to turn off the ventilator," Natasha told Robin.

"Why's that?" Robin inquired.

"Well, we told him that at this point her paralysis is complete, that the only thing keeping her alive is the ventilator. We also told him that her skin and bedsores would only continue to get worse."

ALS

ALS, often called "Lou Gehrig's disease," is a progressive neurodegenerative disease that affects nerve cells in the brain and the spinal cord. The progressive degeneration of the motor neurons in ALS leads to the patient's death. When the motor neurons die, the brain loses the ability to initiate and control muscle movement, and the muscles begin to atrophy from lack of use. In time, as patients lose voluntary muscle action, they become totally paralyzed. As the disease spreads to involuntary muscle movements such as those used for respiration, patients are unable to live without mechanical assistance. Most people diagnosed with ALS eventually die of respiratory failure or pneumonia.

Although ALS affects the body's motor neurons, it does not affect sensory nerves, so that most ALS patients are able to see, touch, hear, smell, and taste. And although the progression of the disease often means that individuals lose almost all voluntary muscle control, some muscles, such as the eyes and the bowels, have been found to be spared or the last muscle groups to deteriorate during the progression of ALS. Because eye muscles are often the last to be lost, the eyes are also often the last means through which a patient suffering from ALS can communicate with others. Using clear panes that have words or symbols inscribed on them, the patient can "point" to what they want or need with their eyes.

ALS does not generally affect cognitive functioning, but 10 percent of ALS patients go on to develop fronto-temporal lobar dementia, which affects both perception and personality. Sufferers of fronto-temporal lobar dementia experience erratic decision making, personality changes, and mood swings. Although only 10 percent of all ALS patients will suffer from this dementia, up to half will suffer from some fronto-temporal lobar degeneration that will have a significant impact on their decision-making capabilities, leading to impulsive or potentially irrational decision making.

Some ALS patients also suffer from pseudobulbar affect—that is, inappropriate laughing, crying, or other exaggerated emotional expression. This symptom results from deterioration of the motor neurons that control those functions, with the brain increasingly unable to subtly control such muscle responses.

MONDAY

Natasha called Robin into her office to inform her that they would be getting a new patient, a Mrs. Haye, who happened to be in a ventilator unit at UniHealth Post-Acute Care of North Augusta, a nursing home facility owned by UHS-Pruitt. Natasha gave the basic details of the case—that the patient had ALS; that the husband, with power of attorney, had made the decision to turn off the ventilator; and that Allie Briggs, the nursing home social worker, would be calling her soon to arrange a meeting with the client. Robin scribbled down the information and was looking forward to meeting with Mrs. Haye.

TUESDAY

The next day Allie Briggs called Robin to report that a Mrs. Haye had been transferred from another ventilator unit to their hospice unit. Because Robin already planned to meet with other patients on the same unit that day, she readily agreed to join Allie in meeting with Mrs. Haye.

Upon entering the room, Allie introduced herself and Robin as social workers and mentioned that Robin was a hospice social worker. Robin noticed that Mrs. Haye's eyes moved when, during Allie's introductions, Allie pointed at Robin. *Someone's still at home*, Robin thought. Despite Bernie's decision to disconnect his wife from the ventilator, he had yet to sign up for hospice support services. The hospice unit would not get reimbursed for any therapeutic help or support until he did so. Mrs. Haye appeared quite frail, with pale skin and dark stringy hair. Because her physical paralysis was nearly complete, she could move only her eyes. But she could no longer blink, and staff had to moisturize her eyes to prevent them from drying out.

Upon returning to the hospice office, Robin stopped to talk with Natasha and Becky about the process of turning off the ventilator.

"How did the meeting with Mrs. Haye go?" Natasha asked.

"It went well, I think. She's pretty frail," Robin reported, "but it's as if she still knows what's going on."

"Why do you say that?" Natasha wondered.

"When Allie introduced me," Robin explained, "Mrs. Haye moved her eyes to look at me."

"Okay, so she can still move a little bit," Natasha acknowledged.

"It looks like she's oriented to self," Robin insisted.

"We can't be sure about that, Robin."

"Well," Robin rejoined, "she might be."

"As it is," Natasha explained, "Bernie has made the decision, considering her physical issues, to turn the ventilator off."

"Well," Robin wondered, "who's going to have to tell her it's being turned off?"

"What do you mean?" Natasha asked.

"I mean, who's going to tell her that the ventilator's going to be turned off? I think she should be told, right?"

"We have to go along with what the power of attorney says and whether he wants us to tell her, for him to tell her, or to not tell her at all."

"And what does he want?"

"We haven't asked him yet. But if he doesn't want her to be told, we're not going to tell her."

"Well," Robin insisted, "I think she deserves to be told regardless because she's still with it; she can still follow commands."

"Well, Robin, we can't prove that," Natasha responded, "without doing CAT scans and other tests. And it's Bernie's decision."

"I'll call Bernie," Becky volunteered, "and see what he wants to do, Robin."

"Alright," Robin agreed. But as she returned to her office, Robin thought, *They're ready simply not to tell her!*

WEDNESDAY

About 9:00 the next morning, Robin came into the office just in time for another meeting with Natasha and Becky.

"Did you talk to Bernie?" Robin asked Becky.

"Yes," Becky reported, "and Bernie says he does not want her to be told. He doesn't want to 'worry' her."

"So," Natasha interjected, "that's what we're going to do."

"But I don't think that's right!" Robin exclaimed. "I don't know her spiritual background. We don't know what she may want; we simply do not know!"

"Robin," Natasha responded, "you're putting your values onto the situation, and you can't do that."

"I don't feel like I am."

"You keep saying 'I, I, I.' But it's about them. It's about Bernie and his wife."

"But what about what the patient wants? We don't know what *she* wants," Robin emphasized.

"I agree with you," Natasha acknowledged, "but we have to do what he says. We simply don't know if she's competent or can communicate her wishes to us."

"She's still with it, though. She has a right to know about her medical care," Robin insisted. Turning to Becky, she asked, "What do you think?"

Becky shrugged and answered slowly, "I don't know, Robin."

"I think she should be told," Robin repeated, turning back to Natasha, "and I'm going to call Pam and ask her what she thinks." Aggravated, Robin quickly left the room to call Pam.

Back in her office, Robin called Pam. But Pam was in a meeting, so Robin told her administrative assistant that she needed to ask Pam a question as soon as possible.

It was nearly 3:00 PM when Pam returned Robin's call. Robin quickly explained the situation and expressed her concern about the need to inform Mrs. Haye.

"Is she signed up for services?" Pam inquired.

"Not yet," Robin acknowledged.

"Well, you need to get that taken care of first," Pam reminded. "Otherwise, we don't get reimbursed for anything." Then, turning to address Robin's question, she asked, "What does the husband say?"

"Becky says that he doesn't want us to tell her and that he isn't going to tell her."

"Well," Pam responded, "I think you guys are making more of this than what it is. I think this is getting blown out of proportion, and I think you're getting too much into this. You just need to go there and support the family."

"Okay," Robin responded, subtle frustration evident in her voice.

After a bit more conversation, Robin said good-bye and hung up the phone. She sometimes thought that Pam was overly concerned with numbers and financials, a sentiment shared by most others in the office, and Pam's comments only seemed to confirm this view. *She only cares that Mrs. Haye isn't yet signed up for hospice services and that we're not yet getting paid!*

After talking with Pam, Robin returned to Natasha's office to tell the others what Pam had said. Becky volunteered that she initially felt okay about not telling Mrs. Haye, but after hearing Robin's objections she didn't know what to do. Natasha remained firm but mentioned that the respiratory therapist did not feel comfortable turning off vents and would instead send a subordinate to do it.

"Then I don't feel I should have to go," Robin said.

"Well, Robin, you can't do that, you just can't give up or not go because if you do that, you'll never get hard cases."

"Well," Robin said, "I just don't think it's right." Despite her reservations, Robin resigned herself to go, if only to help the nursing home staff with anything they might need and to show Natasha that she could handle difficult, challenging cases.

That evening Robin attended class at the University of Georgia. She knew her instructor, Dawn Jarrett, had worked as an oncology social worker for many years and was familiar with end-of-life issues in families. After class, Robin asked Ms. Jarrett about the situation.

As Robin recounted the situation and her concern, Ms. Jarrett asked, "Who is your client, Robin?"

"Mrs. Haye is the client," Robin responded. "I feel she should know. I feel it's her right to know."

"I think she should be told," Ms. Jarrett agreed.

On the way home that night, Robin felt emboldened by Ms. Jarrett's agreement. *So I am right!* While driving, she called Natasha and told her that she had discussed the situation with one of her professors. Robin stressed that Ms. Jarrett had pointed out that because Mrs. Haye was Robin's client, she had a duty to be her advocate.

"That's ludicrous," Natasha responded. "You guys are putting your own values on this case—your own wishes and beliefs—and that's not right. We have to go along with what the power of attorney says. I've seen a lot of things in the hospital that I don't like, but I did them because that's what the power of attorney says." Natasha sounded upset.

"Fine," Robin said reluctantly. "I'm going to talk to another one of my professors, who has a background in law, and see what he thinks."

"I think he'll agree with me, Robin." Natasha said.

Robin said good-bye and hung up the phone. *I hope Dr. Andrews agrees with me.*

THURSDAY

On Thursday, Robin had a daytime class, this time with Dr. Andrews, who had a background in law as well as social work. She explained to him the same things she had explained to Ms. Jarrett the night before.

"I understand your concern, Robin," Dr. Andrews said, "but legally you have to go with what the power of attorney says."

Now Robin was more confused than she had been when she left the hospice office the day before. She respected the opinions of both professors she had talked with, but they had offered contradictory perspectives. *So who's right?* Robin wondered.

FRIDAY

Even before Robin arrived at the office on Friday, Mrs. Haye weighed heavy on her mind. Facing the events of the day, she felt a mix of trepidation and frustration. The previous night she had tried to prepare herself mentally for the day ahead.

When she arrived at 9:00 AM, Natasha was still in the office, but Becky had already left for UniHealth. Natasha informed Robin that Becky had visited Bernie on Thursday to have him sign up his wife for hospice services and to finalize details for turning off the ventilator. Bernie had told Becky that Mrs. Haye's son, Buddy, was on his way down from Virginia and would be arriving later that Friday morning before the final shutoff.

Robin left for UniHealth around 11:00 AM. When Robin arrived, she met with Becky, who told her that Bernie wasn't there yet, despite assuring them he would be there at 9:00. Buddy was already in the room, along with his wife and their two children, ages five and six. It was apparent that Buddy had been crying as he sat at the foot of the bed. Speaking softly, Robin introduced herself to the son and his wife and briefly explained her role.

"I'm here," Robin explained, "to assist with any issues you have as far as burial arrangements or resources for those grieving. I'll try to support you during this difficult process the best I can."

"Thank you," Buddy said simply.

As they stood at Mrs. Haye's bedside, Buddy's wife blurted out, "I believe she should be told what's going to happen . . . because what about her soul?"

You're kidding me, Robin thought. *So the family's divided about this, too?*

"What do you think?" Robin asked Buddy.

Without answering Robin's question, Buddy posed his own. "What would you do?"

"I really can't tell you what to do. Maybe there's a way for you to talk to her without going against your stepdad's wishes, as Bernie wants her not to be told. "

"I'm on the power of attorney, too," Buddy stated.

She gave you power of attorney? Robin wondered silently. *Is this really happening? Now what?! I don't want to create more confusion.*